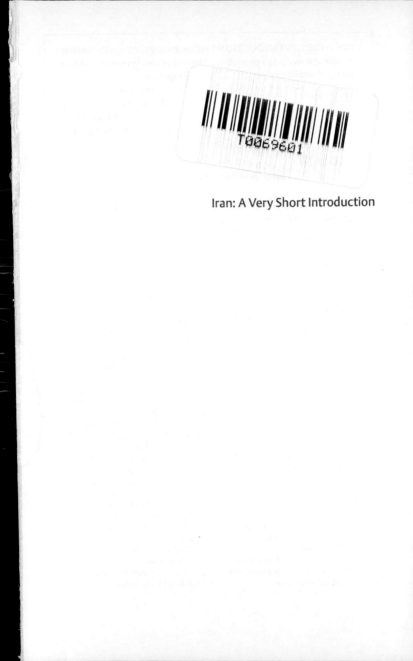

Iran: A Very Short Introduction

Very Short Introductions available now:

Available soon:

For more information visit our website

www.oup.com/vsi/

Ali M. Ansari

IRAN

A Very Short Introduction

OXFORD
UNIVERSITY PRESS

OXFORD
UNIVERSITY PRESS

Great Clarendon Street, Oxford, OX2 6DP,
United Kingdom

Oxford University Press is a department of the University of Oxford.
It furthers the University's objective of excellence in research, scholarship,
and education by publishing worldwide. Oxford is a registered trade mark of
Oxford University Press in the UK and in certain other countries

Published in the United States of America by Oxford University Press
198 Madison Avenue, New York, NY 10016, United States of America

British Library Cataloguing in Publication Data
Data available

Library of Congress Control Number: 2014942173

ISBN 978-0-19-966934-9

Printed in Great Britain by
Ashford Colour Press Ltd, Gosport, Hampshire

For my sister Leila

Contents

Acknowledgements

When I was first asked by OUP to consider writing the VSI on
Iran I had little appreciation of just how difficult the task might
be, not simply in summarizing or distilling ideas that have been
debated, disputed, and above all qualified over several years, but
in not having access to that peculiar comfort blanket beloved by
academics—the footnote! It proved a distinct if thoroughly useful
intellectual exercise which served to clarify my thoughts, and I
hope I have managed to shed some light on the idea of 'Iran'. I am
in sum very grateful for having been given the opportunity to
write this introduction and my thanks extend to the editorial and
production teams for so professionally seeing this text through to
publication. I am likewise grateful to colleagues in the University
of St Andrews and beyond for their engaging and provocative
discussions (long may they continue), and to the energetic
support of my family, most obviously Marjon, whose patience—as
I strove to meet another deadline (rarely alas achieved)—was
truly virtuous!

List of illustrations

List of Illustrations

A note on nomenclature

Mention the words 'Persia' and 'Persian' to anyone in the West and it is likely to elicit a positive response. Word association might result in a discussion of cats, carpets, or, among the more affluent, caviar. Mention Iran and the Iranians, and the response is likely to be more negative with thoughts gravitating towards nuclear confrontation, extremism, and radical Islam. This is ironic given that one motivation behind the decision of the Iranian government in 1934 to insist on the international usage of the native appellation 'Iran' and 'Iranians' for the country and its people, as opposed to the conventional Western use of 'Persia' and 'Persians', was that it would remove the tendency to associate the country with decadence and decay. They would have been sorely disappointed by later developments.

Persia and Persian were the names the Greeks had given to the empire of the Achaemenid dynasty (559–330 BC) that had hailed from the province of 'Pars' in the southern half of the Iranian plateau. This appellation stuck and was inherited by the Romans and subsequently by their European offspring. There is no equivalent native word to describe the inhabitants of the plateau and its hinterland, though it would seem that historically some derivative of *Parsi, Parsig* was in use, and in one particularly famous inscription, the Achaemenid King Darius describes his lineage neatly as Achaemenid by clan, Persian by tribe, and

Aryan/Iranian by people. The term Aryan, and its cognate terms *Eran, Iran,* is generally accepted to have had its origins as a linguistic grouping originating in Central Asia—peoples who spoke Iranian languages—though some have argued that it also denoted freeborn, noble. It has nothing to do with the 19th century European racial classification.

To further complicate matters the language spoken continues to be called Parsi (i.e. Persian) or more commonly Farsi, since following the Arab Muslim conquest in the 7th century AD, and the absence of the letter 'p' in the adopted Arabic alphabet, many words pronounced with a 'p' were simply refashioned with an 'f'. The Iranians subsequently invented a 'p' to address this deficiency, but by then 'Farsi' appears to have embedded itself within the vocabulary and has remained ever since. Persian is an Indo-European language with a basic vocabulary that would be familiar to speakers of European languages, including the words for father (*pedar*), mother (*madar*), brother (*baradar*), and girl/daughter (*dokhtar*). It is this linguistic proximity that in part explains the Iranian cultural affinity with Europe.

The terms 'Persian' and 'Iranian' are not synonymous but they have come to serve as such in foreign usage. This is not an unusual development. The Iranians themselves, for instance, tend to use the shorthand 'Inglisi' (English) to describe Great Britain, and many remain unaware of the distinction or indeed of the contribution of the constituent parts to the wider culture. The same might be said of the concept of 'Persian culture', a term which tends to simplify the complex and multi-layered inheritance it represents, and which often extends far beyond the borders of the modern state.

Chapter 1
Reading Iran

In 2006 Warner Brothers released the film version of Frank Miller's highly stylized graphic novel of the Spartan defence at Thermopylae, titled the '300'. Like all good storytellers Miller was less interested in factual accuracy than with the message he sought to convey, and there was little room for nuance. The protagonists were clear, though there was an added twist to the standard tale of freeborn Spartans heroically defending the 'Western' civilization against the Persian hordes determined to enslave it. In this case it was not sufficient for the Persians to be despotic and 'un-free', they also had to be monstrous. They were not so much 'Immortal' as un-dead, while Xerxes, the original Oriental Despot, seethed with a decadence that could leave the audience in no doubt that he was a 'bad thing'.

Entertaining as the film was, it elicited a harsh reaction from Iranians both at home and abroad and even drew a formal protest from the Iranian government at the UN. Quaint though this protest might have appeared to Western observers, it reflected a deeper anxiety among Iranians that their culture, civilization, and identity had been misunderstood and unfairly maligned by those in the West. Such fears were only reinforced when a leading American negotiator in the nuclear discussions apparently casually told her Congressional inquisitors in 2013 that she was well aware that Iranians had deception in the DNA.

Iran

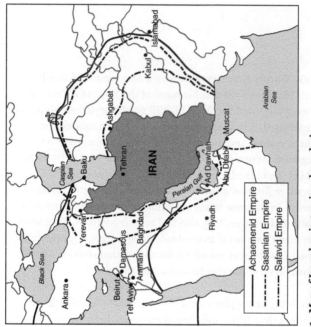

1. Map of Iran showing various boundaries
a. The Achaemenid Empire; b. The Sasanian Empire—
Iranshahr; c. The Safavid Empire; d. Modern Iran

These examples highlight two important contributing factors to any understanding of Iran and the identity of the Iranians: the centrality of history; and the subtle nature of Iran's relationship with the West. An understanding of Iran's history is not only important for the context and frame of reference it provides, but, perhaps more importantly, the light it sheds on the experiences that Iranians consciously claim to share. What Iranians choose to remember is often as important as what they decide to forget, and Iranian governments have had an unhealthy preoccupation with reshaping the past in their own image. The past is therefore a political battleground in which successive governments, political factions, and increasingly the people have sought to position and anchor themselves. Indeed, unhappy with the present and anxious about the future, Iranians spend an awful lot of time contemplating—and occasionally seeking refuge in—their past. Some appreciation of that past and how it affects the present—consciously and unconsciously—is therefore important for any understanding of Iran (see Figure 1).

The relationship with the West is likewise often misunderstood. Coloured as it has been by the antagonism that has characterized Iran's relationship with the United States—and to some extent its allies—there has been a tendency in some quarters, both in Iran and the West, to see the relationship as a continuation of that depicted in '300': fixed, continuous, and with clear moral parameters, even if from the Iranian perspective the roles of slave and freeman would be reversed. This Western relationship is important for a number of reasons not least because it is from the perspective of the West that most readers will approach Iran, even among Iranians themselves. This is a simple consequence of the fact that historical and political writing remains—for the present at least—dominated by the West. But perhaps more interestingly because the West is not a disinterested observer. From the Greeks onwards, Classical, European, and ultimately Western writers have been keen observers of the 'Persians' as they understood the Iranians, both familiar and at times contemptuous but more

3

respectful than many might assume. The Persians, uniquely, form an integral part of the foundation myth of the 'West', and their defeats at Marathon and Salamis (if not Thermopylae) ensured—according to some—the survival of a distinct Western civilization. Much of this to be sure is overblown, but it would be difficult to overestimate the impact of this narrative on the popular consciousness in the West, even if it is rarely these days explicitly stated. After all, athletes, the world over, run marathons.

In reading Iran therefore Western writers approach their subject with considerable cultural baggage, not all of it by any means negative but one that is undoubtedly coloured by an extensive cultural, literary, and occasionally political relationship. It is one in which the Persians nevertheless represent the 'other' in the Western imagination—a civilized other, but a distinct other nonetheless and one whose fortunes are curiously related in such a way that 'Persia' is often held up as a mirror to the West. 'They' are all that we choose not to be, even if they reflect back truths about ourselves that we would rather ignore. The same is of course true of Iran's current perception of the West (traditionally identified with 'Rum' (Rome) and until recently defined as Europeans—literally Franks (*farangi*)—rather than 'Westerners' (*gharbi*)), which, while overtly antagonistic, disguises a much more nuanced relationship than they would care to admit. For all the antagonism on display, Iran's clerical leaders espouse an Islamic *Republic* that owes as much to the ideas of the European Enlightenment as to Islamic law, while its constant condemnation of the materialism of the West (in contrast to its own avowed spiritual purity) sits uneasily with the stark materialism of contemporary Iranian society where cosmetic surgery is aspired to on an alarming scale.

That such stark contradiction should exist should come as no surprise for a society as rich in historical and cultural inheritance as that of Iran. On one level this may be presented as a healthy pluralism, the expression of a dynamic civilization. Yet the distinctions between image and reality are often so striking as to require some further investigation and explanation. All the more so because these contradictions are, more often than not, self-imposed, with the material reality rarely matching the idealistic aspirations. Moreover, there is often a sense that Iranians deliberately seek to maintain these contradictions in a determined bid to defy definition: to maintain that very 'exotic' exceptionalism they are just as likely to protest about in a concerted effort to protect themselves.

If there is one characteristic of the Iranians that Western observers have repeated since the 17th century, it is their apparent propensity for mendacity. Some of this undoubtedly reflected the obsequiousness of courtiers empowered by a poetic language. But the poetry of the Persian language also protected the weak against the overweening power of the state. Outright mendacity undoubtedly existed as it does in all societies, but what the Persian language provided was a facility for ambiguity which allowed the articulate—and anyone versed in a measure of Persian literature—to indulge in verbal acrobatics that neither committed nor condemned. This must have been deeply frustrating to Western interlocutors who simply sought a clear answer but it was an essential defence mechanism for Iranians confronted with a powerful state, limited laws, and few rights. It is a mechanism that exists to this day, and if Iranians use it against the potential depredations of their government so too have successive Iranian governments used it to good effect against powerful foes overseas. If Iranians complain at being misunderstood, the fault in part lies with themselves.

Ambiguity has been, in short, the means by which Iranians navigate the dangers of arbitrary politics, though so pervasive has it become as a social practice that it also serves to justify autocracy. The clarity and decisiveness of the 'leader' is always attractive to those who would rather not make a choice. This absence of clarity is also apparent when we come to define the

Iranians themselves, where the contradictions that exist reflect an unwillingness to choose between competing and often polarized tendencies: tendencies and tensions that run right through Iranian history and are reflected in Persian literature. The tension between, for example, 'Iran' and 'Turan', sedentary and nomad, state and society, and, more recently, the pulls of tradition and modernity. Successful Iranian leaders have, Leviathan like, always been able to reconcile the many tensions and arbitrate between the contending contradictions.

Indeed, perhaps the key to understanding Iran and the Iranians is not to try and define them as one or the other but to see instead how they have sought, through experience and their perception of that history, to navigate a path through that ambiguous and contested middle ground. This brief introduction should thus not be primarily read as a 'History' of the Iranians, but how the Iranian present imagines its past and, in so doing, constructs a thoroughly cosmopolitan, inclusive, and, yes, frequently contradictory identity.

Iran

Chapter 2
Mythology and history

Some two hours outside of the city of Shiraz lie the extensive ruins of the once great ceremonial capital of the Achaemenid Persian Empire. The monumental stone plinth surmounted by pillars and the winged griffins guarding the 'gateway of nations/peoples' have been frequented by curious visitors for centuries, most of whom gazed in wonder at the legacy of majesty and decay. The Greeks called this city Persepolis, the city of the Persians, but the Iranians learnt to know the city by the name 'Takht-e Jamshid', the Throne of Jamshid, one of the great kings of Iranian mythology (see Figures 2a and 2b). This was the name they commonly applied until the 19th century and it remains in widespread use to this day, sitting alongside the more recently adopted, or revived, Persepolis. That the Iranians should have two names for this monument to ancient majesty, and that, more tellingly, they seem to have no desire to replace one with the other, is indicative of their peculiar dual historical inheritance; one mythological and one historical.

Both these narrative strands have had a powerful influence on contemporary identity, and if the mythological strand waned in the middle of the 20th century it has returned with some force in subsequent years, capturing the imagination of both state and society. Even at the turn of the 20th century foreign observers noted, often with a hint of disdain, that the only history most Iranians actually believed in or related to was their mythological

2. a, Line drawing of Persepolis/*Takhte-Jamshid*; b, A view towards the Apadana at Persepolis/*Takhte-Jamshid*

inheritance which charted not only the descent of the first man but subsequently the creation of the kingdom of Iran and its turbulent relations with its neighbours. Only with the latter part of the narrative dealing with the Sasanian monarchs—the last pre-Islamic dynasty—did the mythological narrative flow into a complex interweave of legend and history. The two earlier imperial dynasties, the Achaemenids, and to a lesser extent the Parthians (or more accurately, the Arsacids), had been effectively whitewashed from the narrative and, barring one or two exceptional kings, had been replaced by two mythical dynasties. As a result it is often said that the Iranians had forgotten their history, until Western archaeologists and historians were good enough to remind them. Given the richness of the mythological inheritance, the many truths it contains, and the profound impact it has had on Iranian culture and life, it might be more accurate to say that they remembered it differently.

The historical narrative emerged in the 20th century to provide an alternative competitive strand. Not only did it enjoy the advantage of being the product of 'real' history produced by the *modern* discipline forged in universities, its general thrust was positive and endearing to both Judaeo-Christian culture and the Western narrative in general. Put simply the figure of Cyrus the Great, the great emancipator and liberator of the Jewish exiles from Babylon, was a cult figure in the West long before he was reintroduced to Iranian audiences (Cyrus was a popular name among Puritans and remains widely used in the United States). Cyrus was no pharaoh, he was the Lord's Anointed; one of two messiahs listed in the Old Testament. Unsurprisingly, Iranians, most obviously those intellectuals that were acquainted with Western history and the rigours of the academy, had little problem in adopting and disseminating this narrative even if what we actually knew of this ancient past was more dependent on non-native histories that were not without difficulty. Cyrus, along with his immediate successors, Darius and Xerxes (his son Cambyses was not accorded the same level of rehabilitation), soon became part of a royal 'canon' which most Iranians could willingly look up to, and perhaps most famously, in an echo of Christopher Marlowe's famous verse in *Tamburlaine the Great* ('Is it not passing brave to be a king, and ride in triumph through Persepolis?'), the last Shah of Iran, Mohammad Reza Shah, held a great ceremony and parade in the shadow of Persepolis in 1971 to commemorate 2,500 years of Iranian monarchy.

In order to stress this lineage, the Shah then somewhat abruptly changed the official calendar in Iran in 1976 from a Muslim one dating to the *hijra* (migration) of the Prophet of Islam, Muhammad, from Mecca to Medina, to the purported accession date of Cyrus in 559 BC, a date that effectively added a thousand years to the official calendar. Needless to say this arbitrary change caused a good deal of consternation among Iranians, not least because of the enormous inconvenience it caused to everyday lives and transactions. The religious classes (*ulema*) were unsurprisingly incensed by this affront to Islamic sensitivities, and the Shah's apparent sympathies for the pre-Islamic religion of Iran, Zoroastrianism, but other criticisms were less expected. Indeed for those familiar with Iranian history and mythology, the decision to start the clock with the accession of Cyrus the Great seemed not so much to be an extension of the official narrative of descent, but an abrupt shortening of it.

A myth of descent

Few Iranians today would base the chronology of their state on a mythological narrative which at best would see their history stretch back tens of thousands of years (one early 20th century practitioner calculated a pedigree that would have made the Iranian state/kingdom substantially older than the planet itself!), but it would be difficult to understand the Iranian sense of themselves without some appreciation of the myth of descent that sees the origins of Iran with the creation of the first man. Indeed it is important to recognize that Iranian mythology supports a creation myth independent of its subsequent adoption of Islam, and it is this fundamental aspect which lends weight to the Iranian belief in themselves as a civilization rather than a territorially limited nation. Iranians are of course not unique in possessing a creation myth, but they are perhaps among the few that have retained it parallel to a specifically religious—in this case Abrahamic—creation myth that is sourced to Adam. Adam is the first man and prophet; Kayomars (also pronounced Gayo*mard*) is, in the Iranian narrative, also the first man, but in this case, king. Interestingly, both the words *ādam* and *mard* are in current usage to denote a man although, perhaps significantly, ādam denotes a man of higher status.

Iran's mythological inheritance appears to have been largely transmitted orally (though there is some evidence that a prose version had been collated as early as the 6th century but was in turn subsequently lost and/or fragmented), and it was first written down in the form that we have inherited today by the 10th century eastern Iranian poet Abul Qasem Ferdowsi, who, according to the autobiographical parts of the epic poem he produced, took the better part of his lifetime to write it. And so he might. Not only did Ferdowsi have to collate the extensive stories, he decided to put it all into verse. The fruit of his labours—known to posterity at the *Shahnameh* (*The Book of Kings*, or alternatively *Great Book*—the word *shah* (king) in Persian is often used as a prefix to denote something large, great, and/or majestic), at 100,000 lines is reckoned among the longest poems in history. Though even at this great length Ferdowsi omitted some important mythological narratives that can be sourced to other prose histories compiled by contemporaries. It is nonetheless a vast reservoir of mythological tales, some of which are famous and widely recited, other parts of which remain largely unknown. Crucially, as a poem intended for recitation, it did not require mass literacy for social dissemination.

Despite its title—*The Book of Kings*—and its narrative structured around two (or three depending on how you choose to define them) dynasties, the kings depicted are a decidedly mixed bag ranging from the brilliance of a Kay-Khosrow, to the sheer duplicitous incompetence of a Kay-Kavus. The prefix 'Kay' in this context not only denotes king but also provides the root of the dynastic name—the *Kayanids*, who by this account are the first and the longest-lasting Iranian dynasty, emerging with the creation of Iran and dying with the last of the Sasanians (who saw themselves as Kayanids) with the Arab/Islamic conquest in 642 AD.

The Kayanids are preceded by the *Pishdadian*, sometimes translated as the givers of justice, who are the mythical kings of the entire world, and who busy themselves with taming animals, conquering demons, and introducing mankind to the basic sustenance of life including clothing and cooking. By far the most famous of these early kings is Jamshid (whose 'throne' we have already encountered), who is credited with the ordering of society into classes, the discovery of wine, and the celebration of the Iranian New Year (*Noruz*—the new day), at the spring equinox. So brilliant was Jamshid, so favoured was he by God, that all creatures were subservient to him, be they of this world or the next. Jamshid was in receipt of the divine grace or *Farr-e Izadi*, a concept akin to the divine right but predicated on deeds as well as inheritance. Act justly and the *farr* would remain; act unjustly and it could be lost with terrible consequences for both king and land. This connection with just and good rule would in time be itself forgotten as rulers would turn the concept on its head by arguing that their longevity—however unjustly achieved—proved their possession of divine grace. A concept intended to enhance justice was therefore frequently used to explain despotism. In Jamshid's case, the tale was all too familiar if dramatic. Corrupted by his success, Jamshid aspired to powers well beyond those of a mere mortal. His hubris resulted in his overthrow by the wicked Zahhak—the Arab tyrant—whose oppressive rule lasted 1,000 years until a blacksmith by the name of Kaveh unfurled the banner of rebellion (his leather apron attached to a pole) and restored the rightful king—Fereidoon—to the throne.

There are variations to this narrative, which can be found in the writings of various medieval Iranian authors, that do not make it into the *Shahnameh* itself, especially with regard to the stoicism of the Iranians and the extent of suffering they endured before they finally erupted in an insurrection. Zahhak was secured on his throne through a Faustian pact with the Devil (known in Persian—Zoroastrian—mythology as Ahriman), the price of which was the growth of two snakes from each shoulder which could only be satiated through nourishment with the brains of dead youths. The steward responsible for this grisly meal was so aghast at his task that he swapped one youth for a sheep, the fortunate youngster fleeing to the mountains and, according to the narrative, laying the foundations for the Kurdish people. According to some accounts, Kaveh only rebelled after the authorities demanded that he sacrifice yet more of his sons, and one can only imagine the stoic suffering he had endured before finally deciding to rebel.

Kaveh is nonetheless hailed as the authentic rebel who saw the light and led his people out of darkness. Those on the Left have even interpreted him as the 'first' class warrior, even though, as others have pointed out, his goal was to restore the 'lawful king' and the 'right order'. Kaveh's work done, he then retreats to the margins of the narrative and the centre stage is taken by Fereidoon, the last king of the world, who has three sons, Sām, Tûr, and the youngest, Iradj. Determined to divide his inheritance among his sons, Fereidoon reserves the choicest part—Iran—for the wisest son and sets a test to discover this which Iradj wins. Sām is given the 'West', and Tûr the 'East'. But these two, envious of their younger brother, determine to murder him and in a scene bathed in pathos—and a couplet recited by Iranian children to this day—Iradj pleads for his life to no avail and an aged Fereidoon is confronted with the reality of fratricide. So begins the dynastic struggle between Iran and Turan (the land to the east) and to a lesser extent the West (which in the *Shahnameh* is anachronistically described as Rum (Rome)).

As a mythological and highly personalized account of the subsequent struggles between the empire of the Iranians and its rivals in Central Asia and to the west what is attractive about this particular narrative is that the dispute is a familial one. If the Turanians would eventually morph into 'Turks' the central truth was that these were not understood to be distinct races or peoples, but were in fact all the children of Fereidoon. In practical terms this facilitated an inclusivity and common inheritance that the Western narrative of East and West tended to diminish. Few examples better exemplify this determined inclusivity than the integration of the *Alexander Romance*, which saw Alexander the Great—the great villain of ancient Iranian history—absorbed in the Iranian narrative as the lost son (and rightful heir) of the Persian king and his Greek mother.

The conflict between Iran and Turan also introduced a narrative thread which underpinned much of subsequent Iranian history and identity; a duality with a negotiated ambiguity at its centre. In Iranian mythology, unlike the Western accounts, the centre of gravity shifts eastward, and the ambiguity, as defined by the explicit common inheritance, is more obvious. Indeed the cycle of conflict which shapes Iran and its Kayanid kings is defined not against the West, but against the East in the shape of the Turanians, and while the Iranians are sedentary and urban, the Turanians are increasingly seen as nomadic and rural. The tension is clear but they are more than ever two sides of a single coin, and thus reflections of each other.

This dynamic runs right through the mythology and this anterior rivalry is joined by distinct interior tensions that defined the relationship between the centre and the periphery, personalized in terms of the often fractious relationship between the Shah and his chief warriors, known as *Pahlevans*. These warrior knights, symbolized by the most famous and heroic of their number, Rostam, are to a greater or lesser extent paragons of chivalry against which the various shahs regularly come off worse, certainly with respect to their ethics, which are frequently found wanting. Probably the most famous romance of this heroic part of the *Shahnameh* involves the conflict between Rostam and his son Sohrab. The tragedy that unfolds hinges on the fact that Rostam is unaware that Sohrab is his son and is further reinforced by the tragic nature of the contest that takes place. The ageing Rostam, championing the Shah of Iran, is impressed by the young warrior from Turan who is opposing him. In the first round he is outfought by Sohrab and is compelled to resort to trickery to force Sohrab to desist. The otherwise chivalrous Rostam therefore resorts to distinctly un-chivalrous behaviour to gain the upper hand, while Sohrab remains true to the ethics of his caste. Only on achieving victory, and bringing the young warrior low, does Rostam finally realize that he has killed his son. Like the fratricide noted above, this act of filicide is one of the dominant narrative threads of the *Shahnameh* and is considered by some to reflect the innate conservatism of Iranian society, where the father, albeit inadvertently and tragically, kills his heir. But the tragedy also stresses the theme of heroic martyrdom—reflected in other tales, such as that of Siavosh—which would subsequently be reinforced with Shi'a Islam, and the belief that ultimately one must do the right thing.

The noted scholar of the *Shahnameh*, Dick Davis, has noted that one of its important functions was that of a mirror for princes. It also served more broadly as an ethical guide that provided the essential ideological cohesion for a specifically Iranian culture and world view. It was above all this function—devoid of any political, historical, or indeed specifically religious apparatus—that ensured the durability of the text in circumstances that might be wholly unfavourable to its continued existence. In the aftermath of the Muslim conquest even those who did not adhere to the myth of descent that it espoused could draw on its ethical lessons and moral tales, while modern nationalists could likewise endorse it as a means of social and moral cohesion, if not a *real* history of the Iranians. While it did not accurately describe the *history* of the

Iranians, its value lay in the truths it held about what it *meant* to be Iranian.

This mythology came under assault twice in Iranian history: once in the aftermath of the Muslim conquest when a wholly new narrative of descent from the Prophet Adam was transposed; and secondly in the aftermath of the European Enlightenment and the development of the discipline of history. That it has survived both these challenges, albeit not without adaptation, is testimony to its deep penetration of the social fabric of Iranian society. But this should not disguise the seriousness of the challenges that were posed nor diminish the substantive achievement that was the survival of these distinct myths. No other state that succumbed to the Muslim conquest emerged with its language and mythology not only intact but re-empowered, and the emergence of *New* Persian, now written in the Arabic script, proved a highly effective vehicle for the dissemination of Iranian culture and ideas.

This reflected the cultural confidence of the Iranians built over at least a millennium of dominion, and in practical terms it was achieved by an intellectual-bureaucratic elite determined to keep their traditions alive. They did this not only by redacting oral traditions and translating their works into Arabic but perhaps most importantly by seeking compatibilities between the competing narratives and so maintaining the relevance of their traditions. (A notable absence in the Iranian mythology, for example, is any reference to a great flood, reflecting perhaps that the Iranian myths were products of the Iranian plateau as opposed to the Mesopotamian basin). These were often difficult to achieve, and attempts to argue that, for example, Adam and Kayomars were in fact the same person were accepted as pure speculation. More often than not, historians of this period would simply retain both narratives in parallel, one (Islamic) relating to the history of the prophets, and the other (Iranian) pertaining to the history of kings. Ultimately of course the prophets surpassed the kings, or, as Ferdowsi put it more sublimely at the end of his monumental epic, 'the pulpit replaced the throne'.

Yet, as many of them were at pains to point out, the throne had much to teach the pulpit, and the new bureaucratic elite that administered the Islamic caliphate (and its successors) were enthusiastic purveyors of royal pearls of wisdom about how best to govern a cosmopolitan imperial state. To better serve their new masters, examples were drawn from a range of kings and narratives not all of which were sourced to the *Shahnameh* itself but were drawn instead from other more obscure works. One of the more interesting related to Manouchehr, the grandson of Iradj, upon whose shoulders fell the responsibility of avenging his grandfather. Launching his war against Turan, Manouchehr rallies his people and offers them what amounts to a social contract. Iranian historians described this as the Qutbeh (sermon) of Manouchehr, in a direct allusion to the Muslim pulpit, thereby providing a contemporary resonance and legitimacy to a thoroughly Iranian discourse. The agreement that he offers in an effort to bind himself and his people is a remarkable one that enjoys a relevance to this day. Noting that the people have certain obligations to the king, Manouchehr acknowledges that likewise the king has certain obligations to his people and he adds, somewhat pointedly and for good measure, that no king had the right to tell his people what to wear or what to eat, and that in the administration of justice, it was always better to err on the side of caution, because, 'if at any time he has erred by pardoning, instead of inflicting capital punishment, *this* may be repaired'.

Manouchehr's remarkable 'sermon' was picked up and translated by a number of Western travellers to Iran in the early 19th century, commenting that it provided the best summary of the Oriental mode of government. It has, however, sadly been largely ignored since that initial foray and it would be fair to add that most contemporary Iranians are also unlikely to have heard of it. Indeed, in terms of the administration of justice, there was really

Mythology and history

only one king who stood out in the Iranian consciousness and whose impact on the Islamic world was unusually profound. That king was Khosrow Anushiravan (of the Immortal Soul) alternatively titled 'Dadgar' (the Just), the most famous of all Iran's pre-Islamic kings, to whom most achievements in pre-Islamic Iran are popularly ascribed. Khosrow is richly described in the *Shahnameh* in a series of tales that show him as not only a great and wise ruler, but one who engaged in sage intellectual debate—often with his uniquely talented vizier Bozorgmehr—promoted culture, acquired chess from India, and, above all, administered justice impeccably and universally. So powerful was his particular myth that subsequent rulers sought to collect and apply his various dictums and concocted prophesies by which he had foretold their accession to power. Indeed the name Khosrow itself, like Caesar in the West, soon came to denote Iranian kingship. But Khosrow, unlike Manouchehr, was undoubtedly a real historical figure and it is to this history that we must now turn.

An imperial history

Khosrow I Anushiravan is popularly held among Iranians to be the greatest of the country's pre-Islamic monarchs. Those ancient ruins not ascribed to mythical kings are as a rule credited to Khosrow I, whose reign (531–579 AD) many consider to have been the apogee of the Sasanian dynasty (224–641 AD) whose twenty-second king or King of Kings (*Shahanshah*) he was. A huge amount of what we understand and know of the Sasanian Empire is a reflection of his achievements both in the centralization of the administration and government, and also in the developing orthodoxy of the prevailing Zoroastrian 'state' religion. Although modern historians have tended to deconstruct the Sasanian achievement as reflected in Khosrow's reforms, in the popular Iranian mind-set, the Sasanian Empire is really Khosrow's empire and it is unsurprising that his name has become synonymous with successful imperial rule.

But Khosrow I's achievement also represents the culmination of over a millennium of the Iranian imperium over vast swathes of what we now know as the Middle East stretching from the Oxus to the east to the Euphrates and beyond in the west. The religious and political soul of this empire lay on the Iranian plateau bounded by two great mountain ranges, fluctuating between Pars (Persia) in the west, and Greater Khorasan (literally, the land of the rising sun) in the east—the territorial focus of which has remained remarkably consistent over time. But its economic core lay in Mesopotamia, the land between the two rivers, the heart of *Iranshahr*, the empire of the Iranians, which, remarkably, during the reign of Khosrow I achieved a population density that would not be surpassed till the 20th century.

This Iranian imperium had been founded by a king who had largely been forgotten by Iranians but is now lionized not only as the 'father' of the Iranian 'nation', but as the great liberator of peoples, not least, of course, his own. This king is Cyrus the Great, the founder of the Achaemenid dynasty, which ruled over Iran and much of the Middle East for the better part of two centuries from 559 BC to 330 BC, when the dynasty was overthrown and the empire absorbed by Alexander of Macedon.

What we actually know about Cyrus the Great is largely drawn from Greek sources, further embellished by biblical narratives, in which Cyrus is accorded the distinction of being only the second messiah of the Hebrew Bible (the first being King David), on account of his having liberated the Jews from the captivity in Babylon and allowed them to return to Jerusalem (a good number of them of course never returned but remained firmly within the Iranian world). The Greek sources are likewise sympathetic, though in the case of the Athenian Xenophon, this sympathy took on the character of a prolonged eulogy in his largely fictional *Cyropaedia*, or the Education of Cyrus. Suffice to say that, contrary to the popular image of antagonism between East and West, Persians and Greeks, Cyrus (Persian: Koroush; Hebrew:

Koresh) was a popular figure in the Western narrative, the epitome to a large extent of the philosopher king, who governed as much if not more by consensus as by force. Indeed Greek writers ascribed Persian success under Cyrus as a consequence of his having liberated his people and made them free, while the failure of his successors was put down in part to their having betrayed this particular inheritance.

Cyrus' achievement in uniting the two main branches of the Iranian peoples, the Medes and the Persians, and in creating the first Iranian or Persian Empire, was all the more remarkable, not only for the scale of his conquests stretching from Central Asia through to much of the Near East outside Egypt, but for the manner in which he achieved this, which stood in noticeable contrast to the many conquerors who had preceded him. His was a more subtle, political imperium, and even if his approach did not substantively outlast him, his imperial style clearly had a profound impact on his own people and perhaps more revealingly on those whom he had subdued. Herodotus commented that the Persians regarded Cyrus as a father, since 'the kindness of his heart [was] always occupied with plans for their well being'.

Likewise Cyrus is perhaps the only foreign king in the Bible to be accorded positive feelings, and it is remarkable, given the profound impact Cyrus had on his contemporaries, that the myth of Cyrus was far more durable among his opponents, from whence it entered the Western narrative, than among his own people, when, over time, his legacy was supplanted by the mythical dynasty of the Kayanids; a process of narrative displacement that appears to have accompanied the rise and dominance of the later Parthian dynasty, whose eastern traditions came to supplant those Persian traditions of western Iran. Nonetheless, it was a slow process and Cyrus was not entirely forgotten. A Hebrew version of his name—Koresh—appears in a number of medieval Persian histories, albeit in a somewhat less illustrious capacity: a sub-king rather than *the* King of Kings.

Cyrus' absence from the national narrative has been more than compensated for in the adulation that has since been afforded him by contemporary Iranians. Restored to his proper position by Western archaeologists, modern Iranian nationalists were only too eager to become reacquainted with their ancient monarch whose popularity in the West offered a way for Iran to engage positively with the West. Cyrus facilitated an introduction for Iranians that Egyptians—with their pharaohs—could only envy. What is perhaps most remarkable is not that the figure of Cyrus has become popular with monarchs—eager to acquire some of the lustre—but that he has become embedded in short order within the popular imagination as the 'father of the nation', a title that he would have undoubtedly found strange.

This can be seen simply as the continuation of a process begun with Herodotus and Xenophon and, given how little we know about the real Cyrus, successive generations have been able to embellish the myth with a few choice updates. Not only was Cyrus a liberator, but for the last Shah, and subsequently many ordinary Iranians, the 'Cyrus Cylinder'—a clay tablet discovered in the fortifications of Babylon in 1879 describing Cyrus' conquest of the city—has been anointed, somewhat anachronistically and to the profound irritation of many historians, as the first Charter of Human Rights (see Figure 3). Such has been the popularity of this view that a copy has been deposited at the United Nations in New York. Far from being relegated to the margins by the Islamic Revolution, Cyrus has proved just as popular with Iran's revolutionary elite, who have reinvented Cyrus as an ethical proto-Muslim worthy of the designation 'prophet', while 29 October has been unofficially designated Cyrus the Great day. Indeed in this case the throne has returned to absorb the pulpit. The figure of Cyrus reminds us that in Iran, nothing is clear and everything is negotiable.

The historical Cyrus succeeded in subduing Anatolia, the Near East, Mesopotamia, and much of Central Asia through to the Oxus

3. The Cyrus Cylinder

before he was killed fighting the tribes north of the Araxes River. His body was returned and buried in an imposing tomb in his capital Pasargadae, some two hours from Persepolis, and soon became a source of pilgrimage for friend and foe alike. Alexander the Great was moved when he visited the tomb, which his biographer Arrian described, including an inscription which has come to us via the Greek geographer Strabo: 'O Man, I am Cyrus, son of Cambyses, who founded the empire of Persia and ruled over Asia. Do not grudge me my monument' (see Figure 4).

Cyrus was succeeded by his son Cambyses (*Kambujeye*), who proceeded to add Egypt to the empire but whose reign was cut short by an assassin on account of his despotism, in stark contrast to the charisma of his father. The Achaemenid empire was plunged into its first crisis after which the crown was inherited by a member of a junior branch of the family, Darius (*Dariush*), who in time would also receive the epithet 'Great' on account of his reorganization of the empire around provinces known as *Satrapies*, and the establishment of a sound administration, along with signature projects such as the construction of a canal to link the Nile with the Red Sea and the construction of Persepolis as the ceremonial capital. As Iranians note with some pride, the construction of Persepolis, as evidenced by recent archaeology,

4. The Tomb of Cyrus, Pasargadae

was not achieved through the application of slave labour but through paid labour complete with payments for those who might be injured through their work. Indeed, in contrast to the Greeks, Persian 'freedom', as limited as it might have been, was not sustained by the systematic exploitation of a slave economy.

Darius extended the empire eastwards towards the Indus but is most famous in the West for his decision to extend the frontiers of the empire westwards towards the Aegean peninsula. Greeks in Asia had been living under Persian suzerainty ever since Cyrus had conquered Anatolia and the Ionian coastline, but now, encouraged by their somewhat poorer cousins on the peninsula, the Ionians revolted in a widespread insurrection that resulted in the sacking of the provincial capital, Sardis. The revolt was one of several Darius had to confront as he consolidated his rule and it took several years to finally suppress. Darius then resolved to launch a punitive expedition against the Aegean Greeks in 490 BC, which ended in a fateful defeat on the plains of Marathon. This battle was to become a cornerstone of the Western myth of origins and, while it proved a setback for Darius, it neither changed the balance of power, nor did it affect Darius' domestic position. In

sum, from the Iranian perspective, this was a tactical not a
strategic reverse.

Darius is credited with providing the empire with an institutional
stability that could, to some extent at least, survive the vicissitudes
of dynastic incompetence and excess. Apart from the designation
of provinces and appointment of governors (satraps), which
provided the empire with a degree of centralized and coherent
government, he also standardized weights and measures, coinage,
and, perhaps most importantly, systematized taxation and tribute.
This was not an inclusive imperial system; there was no parity
between the various designated peoples and the Medes and the
Persians held a prime status among all the peoples of the empire
including other Iranian peoples and tribes. There was a hierarchy
of privilege, but what was perhaps most curious was that, for all
the revolts that periodically erupted, the empire that Cyrus built
and Darius organized cohered more through consensus than
coercion. The King of Kings levied troops, as and when required,
and by all accounts retained a limited permanent army—an
imperial bodyguard known to posterity as the Immortals. This
was, in sum, an empire that flourished on the basis of authority,
not raw power.

Perhaps the best expression of this authority was witnessed when
Darius' son and successor Xerxes (*Khashayarshah*) decided that
he would avenge his father's defeat and launched his own offensive
against the Aegean Greeks. In this case, though, Xerxes was not
thinking of a limited punitive strike, but something much more
permanent. In 480 BC, having issued the call to arms from all the
provinces of the empire, Xerxes launched an invasion of the Greek
mainland so huge that there was widespread panic among the
Greek city states. The million-man army of mythology is just that,
but like all good myths it reflected a reality of an unprecedented
invasion force, both on land and sea. Learning from the errors of
his father Xerxes took care to provide extensive logistic support by
gathering an enormous naval force including supply ships that

would shadow the army as it worked its way down the peninsula. Sweeping aside the Spartans at Thermopylae, the Persians moved forward to seize and sack the city of Athens, before finding their progress constrained by a signal naval defeat at Salamis. Hindered by the lack of logistical support from the sea, Xerxes withdrew, leaving a sizeable detachment to complete the conquest. It was finally defeated in one of the largest battles of the era at Plataea, a defeat that put an end to Persian attempts to conquer mainland Greece outright.

Plataea was probably the most decisive of any of the engagements fought between the Persians and the Greeks, yet remarkably it remains the least known and does not appear to rank with Marathon, Thermopylae, and Salamis in the canon of foundational battles for the West. Xerxes was left to nurse his wounds and not inconsiderable pride, though again the defeats were less dramatic for the empire as a whole and Xerxes' successors settled into a much more productive political relationship with the Greeks which effectively saw Pax Persica imposed principally through diplomacy, guile, and money. In the ensuing Peloponnesian War between Athens and Sparta, the Spartans gained the patronage of Persia and the submission of Athens. Indeed, far from being a wholly antagonistic relationship, the competition that undoubtedly existed was bound by a keen sense of mutual respect.

The Persians admired and hired Spartan military expertise; the Spartans for their part often reflected on the chivalry and nobility of the Persians. Perhaps the most famous of these was Cyrus the Younger, Satrap of the West and pretender to the imperial throne. Cyrus was hugely admired by the Greeks, not least the Athenian Xenophon whose *Anabasis* has left us an account of Cyrus' tragic attempt to challenge for the throne with the aid of some 10,000 Greek mercenaries. Following his death at the battle of Cunaxa, Xenophon wrote a touching eulogy on the character of this Persian prince: 'If anyone did him a good or an evil turn he evidently aimed at going one better. Some people used to refer to an habitual prayer of his, that he might live long enough to be able to pay with interest both those who helped him and those who had injured him. It was quite natural then that he was the one man in our times to whom so many people were eager to hand over their money, their cities and their persons.'

This Persian Peace, like all good things, would in time come to an end. Its longevity had depended on maintaining its authority, through good governance and administration among those who were receptive to Persian rule, and through a careful manipulation of local politics among those that might dispute it. The essentially political nature of Persian rule had not been lost on the Greeks who had marched with Xenophon to the heart of the empire and then out again. It had been a struggle, but the fact that it had been possible at all was a reality that puzzled many Greeks. As later social commentators would conclude of Iranian state and society, the 'power' of the King of Kings rested on his continued authority over disparate and divided peoples. The weaker the authority of the king, the greater his determination to reinforce his power by keeping those, both far and near, divided. Such an entrenched policy of divide and rule of course came at a cost to the overall cohesion of the empire. The end of Achaemenid rule witnessed increasing rebellions in the provinces, more fractious politics at home. The accession of a relatively weak king, Darius III, coincided, tragically for him and his dynasty, with a Macedonian hegemony over the Greeks under the leadership of Philip II, and subsequently Alexander.

Alexander the Great's conquest of the Persian Empire over an eight-year period from 334 BC to 326 BC has become the stuff of Western legend. For all the apparent decadence of the empire, the Persian King Darius III was still able to put up a surprisingly robust resistance, and the collapse of the dynasty after three particularly hard fought battles (the first of which saw more Greeks fight for the Great King than for the Macedonian pretender) was never a foregone conclusion. Unsurprisingly Iranians are less enamoured of his exploits, though in a curious and not untypical act of appropriation the figure of Alexander has been inserted into the mythology as a long lost son of the last Achaemenid king. In Iranian mythology, therefore, Alexander becomes Persian in a way that the real Alexander could only have envied. Indeed if Western narratives of Alexander's eastern exploits, reflected as they had been through the political imperatives of Roman imperial historiography, are to be believed, Alexander sought to liberate the East from despotic enslavement through the bounties of Hellenic civilization. The reality was somewhat more complex.

The impetus for conquest had perhaps as much to do with the need to find a common cause to retain Macedonian hegemony over disparate Greeks as it did with any Hellenizing mission; while this mission was probably never quite as unidirectional as later historians tried to paint it. Indeed, if Alexander was corrupted by the splendours of the East, he seemed at times an unusually willing victim, and as some historians have now concluded, Alexander was determined to succeed the Achaemenids, not simply destroy their empire, as witnessed in his enthusiastic adoption of Persian court titles and etiquette. It is this ambivalence in his ambitions that may explain the Iranian tendency to accommodate Alexander within their own pantheon of heroic figures, though more contemporary sources were less forgiving of a conquest which by its very nature was destructive. For the Persians, it was the 'Greeks' that were the barbarians, and the destruction that they wrought on both the physical and spiritual fabric of the empire traumatized the Zoroastrian priesthood in particular, and their condemnation proved especially virulent. Perhaps the most symbolic act of material vandalism came with the 'accidental' razing of Persepolis as a drunken Alexander was persuaded by a courtesan to avenge the burning of the Acropolis by Xerxes some two centuries earlier.

This wanton act of destruction was said to have been much regretted by a sobered Alexander and one can only imagine what might have transpired had he survived beyond his 32 years. Alexander's premature death resulted in the fragmentation of the Persian Empire among his successors with the Seleucids taking the prize of Iran and its immediate hinterland. The century or so of Seleucid rule is regarded as a period of deep Hellenization as reflected in the adoption of names and customs throughout the Near East, to say nothing of the widespread adoption of the Greek language. Though since the Achaemenids had used imperial Aramaic as the language of government rather than Old Persian, the transfer to Greek was probably of less social consequence than some have thought. Certainly the Seleucids barely register in the collective memory, either mythical or historical, and they are largely regarded as peripheral to the national narrative.

This could not be said for the two succeeding dynasties with whom, it may be said, Iranian collective memory truly begins. Curiously the first of these—the Arsacids (Askhanians in Persian), known in Western sources by their tribal affiliation of the Parthians—are less well known and celebrated even though the dynasty ruled, and more importantly helped define Iran, for the better part of 500 years, making them the longest ruling dynasty in Iranian history. It is they, rather than the Achaemenids, who are the harbingers of a distinct Iranian consciousness and mythology. It is perhaps a result of both their longevity and broader social penetration that their 'eastern' Iranian tradition—tracing its roots through to the Kayanids—in time supplanted the 'western' Iranian tradition of the Achaemenids. It is also arguably a reflection of the reality that there was a good deal more continuity than change between the Arsacids and the Sasanian dynasty that ultimately overthrew and replaced them. This continuity is better understood if one appreciates that the Parthian Arsacids were as much part of the Iranian oecumene as the Persian Achaemenids that preceded them and the Persian Sasanians that followed them. Just as the

28

Persian Darius might proclaim himself from the family of the Achaemenes, of the Persian tribe, of the Iranian peoples; so too the Parthian Mithradates might identify himself as of the family of Arsaces, of the Parthian tribe, and of the Iranian people. Multiple identities might prove problematic to the *modern* mind, enthusiastic to establish neat categories; but it is worth considering that such layered identities have been the norm rather than the exception and they certainly have rarely been a problem for Iranians.

Parthia had been a province of the Achaemenid Empire located in the north-east where the Iranian plateau meets the Central Asian plains. The Parthians had been largely nomadic and excelled in cavalry warfare, most famously, though not exclusively, light cavalry horse archers. Their emergence as an independent power is usually dated to the mid-3rd century BC when the eponymous founder of the dynasty, Arsaces I, seized control of Parthia from the Seleucids, though it would not be until the following century that Arsacid domination of the majority of the Iranian heartlands would be established, with the frontier stretching from the Indus to the Euphrates. Although Arsacid control over these territories was often fluid, it is essentially from the 2nd century BC that the recognizable form of *Iranshahr* (the empire of the Iranians) takes shape bordered by the Indus, the Euphrates, and the Oxus, and the Caucasus in the north-west. The most fluid and contested frontiers, interestingly enough, are the north-east and north-west—Turan and Rum in mythological terms.

The Arsacids emerge from within a Seleucid context, reflected in their early use of the term Philhellene on their coins, and there was little indication that they saw themselves as successors to the Achaemenids. But over time the Hellenic influences gave way to more distinct Iranian cultural norms, perhaps most clearly expressed in their religious and political practices—including the assumption of the title King of Kings (*Shahanshah*). Under the

Arsacids the title appears to have implied a position of *primes inter pares*, that is that the Arsacid Shah was a king over other kings denoting a much more confederal and decentralized approach to government, if not feudal as some have sought to describe it. This was in effect an aristocratic government in which leading families contributed to government and the power of the monarch waxed and waned according to the relative power of these noble families. One of these families, the Suren, became especially notable in the ensuing wars against an expanding Roman Republic and a good deal of the written information we have about the Arsacids comes from Roman writers. The princes of the Suren clan were amongst the most powerful of aristocratic families able to raise a host of some 10,000 cavalry, and had the privilege of performing the act of coronation.

In 53 BC the Roman triumvir Crassus, fresh from crushing the slave revolt of Spartacus and anxious to match the achievements of his colleagues and rivals Caesar and Pompey Magnus, sought glory in the East. Disdaining advice to seek the protection of the mountains against the Parthian superiority in cavalry, Crassus determined to march through the desert to the heart of Mesopotamia. He was caught on the plains of Carrhae by the Suren's detachment of heavy armoured cavalry, who contained the legions while the light cavalry archers rode at will and peppered them with arrows. It was the greatest catastrophe to befall Rome since the defeat at Cannae and served notice to the Romans that the Parthian Empire was a rival worthy of respect. So much so that Augustus later made great play of his peace treaty, which ensured the return of the captured eagles, presenting it as a diplomatic triumph worthy of military accolades. As for Crassus, his defeat and death at the hands of the Suren was regarded by the Greek historian Plutarch as the just consequence of his vulgar hubris, though his posthumous humiliation was perhaps an act of hypocrisy too far. The Suren had made much play of the pornographic literature discovered in Crassus' baggage train, noting that even in battle the Romans could not dispense with such material. In what might be considered the first distinct Orientalist/Occidentalist commentary in which the other side is perceived as sexually decadent, Plutarch did not deny Crassus' vulgarity, but added for good measure that the Suren's ample coterie of concubines who accompanied him everywhere was not much better.

In the long run, as with Hannibal's victory at Cannae, the defeat at Carrhae did not alter the strategic balance of power, but the immediate consequences were undoubtedly dramatic and a matter of great anxiety in Rome, since for a brief period Roman power collapsed in the East and Iranian armies once again reached the Mediterranean, even capturing Jerusalem. It was left to Mark Antony to restore Roman fortunes, much assisted by the fact that internal political squabbles ensured that the Parthian king was unable to regularly field armies in the West. The Emperor Trajan proved to be the most successful in temporarily extending the imperial frontier down to the Persian Gulf, but on the whole an uneasy balance of power existed, with the contest focused on primacy over the Kingdom of Armenia, which had in the first century AD acquired a cadet branch of the Arsacid dynasty for itself. Perhaps the most interesting development in this period lay not in the political sphere but in that of religion, as varieties of Christianity and Zoroastrianism—not always, it might be added, entirely distinguishable—competed for the souls of the Near East. This religious competition was to take a more distinctive political hue when heterodoxy increasingly gave way to orthodoxy and the rival 'churches' sought the patronage of the imperial powers of the day.

If Christianity had to wait for the conversion of Constantine in the West, the Zoroastrian priesthood, the Magi, were to find their own patrons somewhat sooner with the emergence of the Sasanians. The Sasanians are the third of the great pre-Islamic imperial dynasties and might be considered the most influential in the shaping of the idea and territoriality of Iran. Indeed it is to them that we owe the very idea of Iran as a distinct political concept, drawing on an amorphous if rich inheritance bequeathed to them by the Parthians and transforming it into a political and cultural idea of profound consequence for the future. The idea of Iran is arguably their greatest legacy. That the influence and knowledge of the Sasanians should be greater than those of their immediate predecessors—whose longevity was greater—is a reflection of their relative proximity in historical terms: the influence that the dynasty, and particular kings such as Khosrow I, had on both the Muslim and Iranian imagination, along with the efforts they themselves took to protect their legacy, and of course the simple reality that they represented the culmination of an imperial project and civilization that would never be the same again. Nostalgia is a powerful catalyst to memory.

Ardashir, the founder of the Sasanian dynasty, emerged from the petty nobility of Persia in the 3rd century CE to overthrow the ruling Arsacids in a succession of battles and establish a new 'Persian' dynasty. His immediate ancestors, back to the eponymous Sasan, were according to some sources priests or protectors of the shrine of the cult of Anahita in Istakhr, near to the ruins of Persepolis. The Sasanians themselves claimed to be the legitimate heirs of a royal tradition and divine grace (*Farr-e Izadi*) that had been usurped by the Arsacids. Just which royal tradition this was is a matter of some speculation among modern historians, though the emerging consensus is that far from seeing themselves as heirs to the Achaemenids, they considered themselves heirs to the Kayanids. This may seem strange given their own origins within Persia proper and their proximity to major Achaemenid monuments, and it is not at all clear that memory of the Achaemenids had been completely erased, but Kayanid origins reflect not only the profound influence of half a millennium of Arsacid rule, but also the importance of the Zoroastrian priesthood to the emergence and legitimacy of the Sasanians.

From the Roman perspective, the change in dynasty was an event of consequence. The Romans, like the Greeks before them, were now confronted by 'real' Persians whose modus operandi was a good deal more disciplined, zealous, and aggressive than they had been used to. Moreover there was an impression that the new King of Kings did not see himself as a first among equals, but very much more in an imperial mould. Ardashir I launched the initial assault on Rome's eastern frontier, but it was his son Shahpur I who was to provide the real shock to the Roman imperial system. Following in his father's footsteps Shahpur won a devastating victory at Edessa in 260 CE and captured the Roman Emperor Valerian in the process—the first time a Roman emperor had been captured in war. Shahpur was sufficiently aware of the magnitude of his victory that he made sure posterity would not forget it by commissioning an impressive rock relief at *Naqshe-Rostam* (literally the picture of Rostam, the traditional name ascribed to the monument) near Persepolis, as well as, it now appears, minting coins to commemorate the triumph far and wide. This rock relief (see Figure 5), along with the Cyrus Cylinder, and the tomb of Cyrus at Pasargadae, has become one of the signature monuments of their ancient heritage for many contemporary Iranians. In a somewhat mediocre present, it is a salutary reminder of bygone glories, when the West was not so dominant.

Nearby, in a cube structure known to posterity as the Kaba of Zoroaster, Shahpur took pains to describe his dominion in the three imperial languages, Middle Persian, Parthian, and Greek. Here he notes that he is King of Kings of Iran and an-Iran (i.e. non-Iran), before listing the list of provinces included in this somewhat expansive designation. Alongside Shahpur's inscription, there is an extensive inscription from Kartir, the chief Zoroastrian priest or Magi/Mobed. Just as Shahpur is the King of Kings, Kartir describes himself as the Mobed of Mobeds, in other words the head of the priestly hierarchy. In this accompanying inscription, the importance of the Zoroastrian church and the priestly class within it to the Sasanian Empire is left in no doubt, and even if Kartir is indulging in a little bit of self-promotion, it is clear that there is something distinctive about the Sasanian Empire.

5. A youthful author at *Naqshe-Rostam*, near Persepolis

Counselling his son about the nature of power, Ardashir I is credited with stating, 'Know that Kingship and religion are twin brothers; there is no strength for one of them except through its companion, because religion is the foundation of kingship, and kingship the protector of religion. Kingship needs its foundation and religion its protector, as whatever lacks a protector perishes and whatever lacks a foundation is destroyed'. This sentiment regarding the centrality of religion to the Sasanian project is echoed in the 'Letter of Tansar', Kartir's predecessor during the rule of Ardashir, who admonishes a recalcitrant Parthian noble for not submitting to the new order by reminding him that Ardashir restored the true faith abandoned by the decadent Arsacids, and that he should never forget that 'church and state were born of the one womb, never to be sundered'. Both these accounts date from the later Sasanian period and project backwards an orthodoxy that probably had yet to develop, but they do nonetheless indicate the importance of religion to the Sasanian state. Indeed Ardashir goes so far as to argue that religion has primacy, 'because religion is the foundation and kingship the pillar, and the lord of the foundation has prior potency over the entire edifice as against the lord of the pillar'. It should not come as any surprise that Ardashir's conception proved popular among the Islamic dynasts who followed, and, perhaps more surprisingly, among proponents of the centrality of religion to politics in Iran to this day.

The belief of many Iranians that the Sasanian state was a powerful centralized structure in which religion played a vital sustaining role has always lacked a secure foundation in the historical record. Ironically this political mythology, which was in large part created and promoted by the later Sasanians themselves, most obviously Khosrow Anushiravan, helped sustain the legacy of the empire long after it had fallen, as different successor states sought both to emulate and justify their own policies on the basis of apparent historical authenticity. But this authenticity has been disputed, in part because the Sasanians were much more obvious successors to the Parthian Arsacids than they would have liked us to believe, but also because the relationship between religion and state was a good deal more fractious than they sought to project. This by no means diminishes the legacy of the Sasanians: indeed, seeing them as part of an imperial continuum stretching back at least to the rise of the Arsacids in the 3rd century BC reinforces that legacy by emphasizing its complementarity. But it is also true that the nature of Sasanian government and its legacy are more complex and interesting than is commonly appreciated. A good example relates to religious policy.

Zoroastrianism

We should pause at this stage to reflect on the influence and impact of Zoroastrianism as the most prominent religion of the Iranian peoples and certainly the faith publicly espoused by succeeding imperial dynasties. The first thing that must be appreciated is that Zoroastrianism as understood today is a product of late antiquity, specifically the attempts by the late Sasanians to encourage an orthodoxy and of Iranian Zoroastrians following the Arab Muslim conquest to redact an oral tradition and both protect and explain the faith confronting the most serious challenge to its dominance. Even the term 'Zoroastrianism' is largely a later construction so as to refocus the faith around its own 'Prophet'; in contemporary terms the religion was known as 'Mazdaism', or simply the good religion (*beh-din*). Nonetheless, and accepting the debates around the rationalization of the faith, it is generally agreed that Zoroastrianism in all its heterodoxy played an important role in shaping the Iranian world view—such that it has been argued that the term Iran itself was developed in the Sasanian era as a cognate term to identify those of the 'good religion'—and that its central tenets came to have a profound influence on the development of the Abrahamic faiths that eventually supplanted it.

Classical authors tended to believe that Zoroaster lived some time in the early 6th century BC, but it is now generally agreed that he lived much earlier, some time between 1200 and 1000 BC, probably in eastern Iran and the area now shared by Iran, Afghanistan, and Turkmenistan. He is also generally regarded as a reformer rather than a prophet in the biblical sense, and his function was to search for and explain the divine purpose, rather than to act as a messenger of the divine will. In this sense, there is something of the mystic about the figure of Zoroaster, and the pursuit of knowledge, esoteric or otherwise, and the promotion of 'good' are central characteristics of the faith. As a reformer, Zoroaster took the folk religion of the day and began a process of rationalization, which saw a clear distinction between good and evil.

This fundamental duality—which Nietzsche would later argue was the moment when morality was introduced into the world—and the explanatory framework for its emergence and relationship to the material world, were to have a profound consequence on religious ideas. For Zoroaster and the Mazdayan religion that developed, the struggle between good and evil was characterized in the struggle between light and darkness, the Wise Lord and creative being, Ahuramazda, who brings harmony and moderation, against the falsehood and destructiveness of Ahriman. This was not a cosmic conflict to which mankind was an observer and occasionally a victim. For Zoroaster, mankind was created to help Ahuramazda in his struggle and therefore (and crucially) was a participant. Moreover Zoroaster did not simply project a concept of time that was linear, he outlined an *end* of times when good would finally triumph over evil. To this day Iranian children are reminded of the simplicity of Zoroaster's injunctions, to do good deeds, think good thoughts, and speak good words.

The dualism of the religion was embodied in the notion of a dual creation. For all that was good in creation, Ahriman sought to create something evil, and in the struggle that was ensuing, each side could draw upon both spiritual and material hosts. Among the ideas that were developed within this cosmology were the concept of a divine spirit, the resurrection, angels, and, perhaps most interestingly, the notion of spiritual messiahs, who would intervene on behalf of the Wise Lord. Zoroastrian tradition posited three such saviours, the last of which would come at the end of time. All were to be born of virgins though they were impregnated by bathing in lakes that had preserved the seed of Zoroaster, rather than the 'Holy Spirit'. This messianic tendency in Zoroastrianism was to have important consequences not only for the development of religion but for political life in general. It undoubtedly contributed to and reinforced a belief in, and need for, a saviour. In Zoroastrian tradition this was symbolized by Fereidoon's overthrow of Zahhak, who, before he was anthropomorphized in the Iranian tradition into a man with two snakes, had been represented as a great dragon—a beast. In the historical tradition, the first such saviour was Cyrus, who of course was accorded messianic attributes in the Old Testament.

The parameters of the faith aside, it is less clear to what extent Cyrus and his successors actually adhered to the doctrines being outlined, other than in a broad ethical sense. The Achaemenids do invoke the name of Ahuramazda, and in an especially popular site near Hamadan, there is an inscription in which Xerxes thanks and praises Ahuramazda not only for his dominion, but also for creating happiness for the world. Similarly his father Darius in another inscription beseeches Ahuramazda to protect the empire from falsehood or the 'great lie'. But in alluding to the fact that Ahuramazda is the greatest of all the gods, Xerxes draws attention to the fact that the strict dualism associated with Zoroaster's apparent reforms was not necessarily adhered to, and certainly the practice of not polluting the earth with the dead does not appear to have been practised by successive kings who chose instead to be entombed, not least of course Cyrus himself. If the Achaemenids were eclectic practitioners of the faith, then the Arsacids appear to have been considerably more relaxed, with the growth in the cults of various sub-deities such as Mithra (*Mehr*), and it was arguably this louche approach to the doctrines of the faith that lost them the support of the Zoroastrian priesthood.

If the Sasanians sought to project themselves as guardians of the good religion, they too appear to have had a flexible attitude to its doctrines, though here perhaps the belief in regular renewal through the appearance of a saviour may have helped in opening the doors to heterodoxy. Two schisms were particularly important and pregnant with consequences for the future. The first occurred during the reign of Shahpur I. This was the rise of a preacher by the name of Mani and the foundation of Manichaeism, an ostensibly new religion born of the duality of Zoroastrianism, though one that stressed the esoteric and spiritual over the material, ascribing all that was wicked to the material world and all that was good to the spiritual: a form of duality that was at odds with mainstream Zoroastrian teaching. Mani sought to bring together in his new religious paradigm the three dominant faiths (as he saw it) of the time: Zoroastrianism, Christianity, and Buddhism. This universal inclusivity proved attractive to Shahpur, who, surprisingly for an apparent guardian of orthodoxy, chose to support Mani. It was only some time after Shahpur's death that his successors were persuaded to crush what was increasingly defined as a heresy (itself a good indication of the orthodox direction of travel). Forms of Manichaeism were to prove popular in the Roman Empire, though with greater distance came greater variance from the religion that Mani himself sought to promote.

Much more serious for the stability of the Sasanian Empire itself was the challenge posed by a radical religio-political thinker by the name of Mazdak at the turn of the 6th century AD. Mazdak has been hailed by some modern thinkers as the first (proto-) communist by virtue of the fact that he argued for a drastic reordering of economic relations with a view to imposing common ownership of all things, including wives. This last element may have been a slur to denigrate Mazdak's project which initially, and surprisingly given its radical egalitarian interpretation of social and economic relations, enjoyed the support of the then king, Kavad. It is in fact difficult to know quite how widespread the Mazdakite rebellion was since the Sasanian state was not unduly constrained by it and it may be that subsequent writers, both Sasanian and Muslim, exaggerated the threat posed to legitimate political and religious centralization. Certainly later Muslim writers would use Mazdak as *the* case study of heresy and its detrimental effects on state and society.

The Mazdakite religion was to be ruthlessly suppressed by Kavad's son Khosrow Anushiravan, who used the rebellion to construct an altogether more coherent, centralized and orthodox empire. Khosrow's I's settlement appears to have been very much the exception rather than the rule. Indeed Zoroastrianism was probably characterized more by its fluidity than its rigidity, and what we might now term heresies appear to have flourished especially in the less accessible parts of the empire. If some had chosen a more polytheistic reading of the faith, others had moved in the other direction seeking a primordial creator (Zurvan) from whom both Ahuramazda and Ahriman had emerged. This was not the dualism of orthodoxy and was likewise supported and tolerated by a variety of monarchs including those from the Sasanian dynasty.

For all the orthodoxy projected by the Sasanians, Zoroastrian heterodoxy was probably more prevalent particularly in those areas distant from the court or indeed the Persian heartlands. Moreover, as the rise of Manichaeism suggests, there was a greater receptiveness to religious beliefs beyond the Zoroastrian traditions, most obviously Christianity, which was not only officially recognized within the empire (Nestorian Christianity) but may have acquired converts in the imperial dynasty itself. It may have been the very heterogeneous nature of religious life in Sasanian Iran that encouraged Khosrow I to stress the orthodoxy of the Zoroastrian faith. But in drawing up new boundaries and effectively changing the rules, Khosrow simply pushed these 'heresies' to the margins of the empire, both politically and geographically. Significantly, Khosrow was in the process of extending these frontiers, these margins of empire, with consequences he could not have foreseen, towards the Arabian Peninsula.

The shadow of the ancients

Ancient—pre-Islamic—Iran looms large in the Iranian consciousness. Part of it has been undoubtedly invented, a great deal reimagined—there is a nostalgia for the past among contemporary Iranians that is more romantic than real (see Figure 6). But it would be unusual if a state and culture that existed in dominion for the better part of a millennium did not leave some imprint on the collective memory of those who lived within its cultural confines, or indeed cast a long shadow on its political successors. Even if they had wanted to distance themselves from this inheritance it would have been difficult to achieve this, but the reality was that few wanted to discard the past, and many went in search of it. Both language and culture proved particularly difficult to dislodge, and if each went through multiple metamorphoses, the traces of the past remained remarkably durable, with key linguistic and cultural practices continuing down the generations.

As for the idea of Iran itself, in its earliest, Achaemenid manifestation, 'Aryan' and its cognate 'Iran' were probably broad linguistic categories denoting speakers of Iranian languages; the Parthian Arsacids coming from beyond the Persian heartlands gave further impetus to the idea of Iran, imbuing it with a cultural depth, while the Sasanians completed the edifice by politicizing it. The sense of Iran as a territorially delimited political state was a legacy of the Sasanians, and they worked hard to build on their own inheritance and reinforce it for the future. They achieved this in part by developing their own sense of history with a

6. One of the signature capitals that adorned the columns at Persepolis, now adorning the tailfin of the national airline, Iran Air

fully-fledged myth of origins and descent that would ultimately be narrated into the epic poem that is the *Shahnameh*.

The legacy of the ancient world for modern Iran can be discerned in four distinct areas. (1) Language: Old Persian and Middle Persian (Pahlavi) flowed inexorably towards New Persian. This would emerge out of the Arab Muslim conquest adopting the new Arabic alphabet to penetrate further than ever before to become the lingua franca of the eastern Islamic world. (2) Religion: a distinct religious tradition built around what we now identify as Zoroastrianism which brought with it ideas about life and the cosmos that would have a profound influence on broader religious thought and practices. (3) History: a myth of origins and descent which would help establish Iran as a distinct civilization. All of which contributed to (4), a distinct culture and ethical world view, which enjoined at its heart an unswerving adherence to an idea of justice.

Contemporaries were repeatedly impressed by the material and intellectual wealth of the 'Persians', such that even the Prophet

Muhammad is reported (at least according to the Iranians) to have pronounced that, 'if knowledge were suspended in the highest heavens, even then the Persians would attain it'. Little wonder that the Iranians enjoyed a cultural confidence and sense of themselves that most could only envy, but which occasionally and dangerously tipped over into hubris. Perhaps this legacy and cultural confidence is best exemplified by the continued use of a distinct solar calendar which has the new year (*Now Ruz*/new day) on the spring equinox (20/21 March); a festival that is rooted in the ancient, Zoroastrian, past, and celebrated to this day. It is in truth an echo, which remains loud, clear, and remarkably vivid.

Chapter 3
Iran and Islam

In 1979 the Islamic Revolution erupted in the Iranian body politic, overthrowing the monarchy and transforming Iran's relations with the outside world. A state that had hitherto appeared to be marching down the path of 'secular modernity', albeit with an authoritarian face, now seemed to be turning its back on progress with a reactionary revolution that sought to impose a distinct, and somewhat innovative Islamic theocracy, albeit now with a democratic veneer. For Westerners who had come to know Iran over decades the revolution proved to be something of a shock to the system. It was not that people had been unaware of the importance of Islam to Iranians or indeed of the limitations of the autocratic monarchy established by Mohammad Reza Shah; but they appeared by all accounts to have both misread the direction of travel and also the sheer centrality of Islam to Iranian identity. In truth many Iranians had likewise been wrong-footed by the pace and nature of the change. The trauma of revolution was compounded by an intellectual bewilderment that demanded answers, and unsurprisingly some of the answers that emerged in the heat of revolution proved as dramatic as the experience of political upheaval itself. According to some, Islam not only contributed to Iranian identity, it *was* Iranian identity, to the extent that some speculated that Iranian-ness (or perhaps more accurately, Persian-ness) was an entirely Western construct imposed upon a quintessentially Muslim nation.

Such drastic reassessments did not survive reality for very long, but it was certainly the case—and arguably continues to be the case—that much of Iranian history was reassessed through an Islamic lens in part to try and help explain a revolution that most found incomprehensible. To some extent this was a necessary antidote to the monarchy's desire to emphasize an imperial continuity but this act of historical rebalancing soon took on imperial pretensions of its own. Not least because the new authorities, including the new leader of the Islamic Republic, Ayatollah Khomeini, were clear in their instructions that a new, politically correct, historical narrative needed to be constructed. One of the functions of this new narrative was to diminish the past in order to stress the dramatic nature of the revolutionary rebirth. An obvious target was the system of monarchy that had just been overthrown. The purpose was not simply to diminish its role and influence, to decry its policies as alien to Islamic Iranian culture, but also to show that the difficulties that might now be encountered by the youthful revolution were the consequence of a poisoned inheritance. Of course, and with no little irony, in using the 'monarchy' as a foil for the problems they encountered, those who came to overthrow it themselves reinforced a narrative of continuity that had little historical foundation.

Naturally the project was to reach far further than the immediate past. The aim was to provide a narrative of descent that was essentially Islamic and Abrahamic in its origins. Mythology was all well and good, but it was just that, mythology, while pre-Islamic Iran from the Achaemenids onwards was interesting but irrelevant. What really mattered was Iran's Islamic history and heritage. It did not take long for even this attempt at radical revisionism to stumble. If researchers were sent forth to investigate Islamic Iran, they were still focused on an entity, cultural or otherwise, that was identified as 'Iran', and it did not take long for the emphasis of the research to stress the important contributions of Iranians to Islam, which slowly but surely established the centrality of the Iranian experience to the narrative of Islam.

It soon became apparent to the authorities that it was not Iranian narratives that were becoming Islamized, but the idea of Islam itself that was becoming Iranianized. It helped of course that Iran adhered to the minority branch of Islam, Shi'ism, whose geographic spread largely coincided with the traditional boundaries of Iranshahr. But this process went even further than the expression of a distinct 'national' pride. Researchers who investigated and rewrote the history of early Islam and its spread throughout the territories of Iranshahr—in an echo of those Christian historians who sought to illuminate the context of Republican Rome—soon discovered that far from being simply decadent and ripe for spiritual rebirth, Sasanian Iran left a profound legacy and inheritance for her successors. Not for the first, or indeed last time, 'captive Persia would take prisoner her conquerors'.

Conquest

The rise of Islam had taken place in the context of the last great war of antiquity. The cycle of wars between Sasanian Iran and its Roman/Byzantine rival to the west had taken an unusual turn by the end of the 6th century AD. Facing rebellion at home Khosrow Anushiravan's grandson, also named Khosrow, had sought refuge and support at Constantinople. The Byzantine Emperor Maurice agreed, only to be overthrown in turn by his own rival, providing Khosrow with an excuse to launch a war against Byzantium in aid of his former patron. Unlike previous wars, however, this offensive was not a raid, nor an attempt to redress boundaries, but a full-scale attempt at conquest of the 'West' not seen since Achaemenid times. It is unlikely that Khosrow II—known to posterity as 'Parviz' (the Victorious)—had the Achaemenids in mind, but recent archaeological excavations have shown that the Sasanians launched their invasion in 602 AD with a view to staying and administering their new territories, seizing Jerusalem (and carrying away the True Cross) and Egypt, as well as Anatolia to the gates of Constantinople itself.

The conquest was eventually undone by the skill of the new Byzantine Emperor Heraclius, who launched a daring raid from the Caucasus into the heart of Mesopotamia, threatening the Sasanian capital of Ctesiphon itself in 627 AD. Fearing collapse, the Sasanian aristocracy overthrew their once victorious monarch and plunged the empire into a prolonged succession crisis. There is little doubt that Heraclius' bold move took his opponents by surprise, unleashing political tensions that had clearly existed for some time, but some historians have conjectured that Khosrow II's imperial adventure unravelled so quickly because the empire found itself attacked not only by Rome but by Turan—the East—and that this proved Khosrow's undoing. Whatever the immediate causes of the dramatic reversal of fortune visited upon Khosrow, it was as nothing compared to the catastrophe that would soon befall the Sasanian Empire as a whole. Within twenty years the entire empire would succumb to an onslaught by followers of a new faith—proclaimed by a new saviour, the Prophet Muhammad—who would sweep all before them and incorporate the Iranian world into a Muslim caliphate, from whence something quite new would emerge. It was, as Ferdowsi himself would have said, the waning of one civilization and the birth of a new. But how new?

Depending on one's religious leanings in Iran, the Arab Muslim conquest was either profoundly positive for the future of the country, or a dramatic disaster. Either way, the conquest marked a break that was so complete that it led ultimately to the emergence of something quite new. Some, now as then, have been enthusiastic about this turn of events; others, now as then, have hungered to discover and recover that which was apparently lost. Yet, perhaps both these interpretations have been wide of the mark. Just as the Sasanian Empire could not be considered 'centralized' by modern standards, so too the Arab Muslim conquest was probably not quite as dramatic or as complete as subsequent histories have sought to suggest. Iranshahr was vast, stretching from the Euphrates through to Central Asia. The fall of the dynasty was relatively rapid, though it still took the better part of a decade, but the conquest and pacification of the empire itself was a much more prolonged affair. All the more so because the invading armies cannot have numbered more than tens of thousands. The conquest was therefore, by necessity, far more piecemeal and sporadic than historical distance pretends, with much co-option of local lords and dynasts—the local kings—who were effectively left to their own devices, including the practice of their own religion, as long as they kept the peace and paid the required tribute. Indeed one historian has noted that by the time the Muslim armies had reached Central Asia they were majority Persian speaking.

Recent research has suggested that while the Arabs seized the rich and fertile areas of Mesopotamia relatively quickly after the decisive victory of Qadisiyya, their penetration of the Iranian plateau was much slower and hard fought with especially tough fighting in the Persian heartlands, as well as further east in what would now be Afghanistan and the mountainous areas of the Caspian littoral, where local dynasts were effectively left to their own devices. The Arabs' principal areas of influence and control lay across the trade routes from Ctesiphon to the north-east and were in the main urban rather than rural. The consequence of this was that there were huge parts of the country that remained relatively untouched by the conquest to the extent that conversion to Islam took several centuries to affect the majority of the population. One should not exaggerate the extent of the continuity, and certainly by the 10th century AD there was a clear realization, as reflected in the redactions of religious and historical texts, that the past needed preserving, otherwise all might be lost. But the slow and somewhat less dramatic nature of this transformation meant that much more would be absorbed from the past into the renewed and reinvigorated cultural body politic.

This cultural absorption was further eased by a number of other factors. In the first place, Iranshahr was absorbed wholesale into the new caliphate. The heirs to the Sasanian dynasty itself fled eastwards towards China (from where they made a number of attempts to retake their patrimony), but other than a limited migration of some Zoroastrians to India, where they became known as *Parsis* (i.e. Persians), there is little evidence of any other significant population displacement. Unlike Byzantium which lost the Near East but retained Anatolia, there was nowhere for the Iranians to go, to say nothing of the fact that for many, as indicated above, there was little reason for them to go. For most of the population, existing outside the political or religious elite, life went on as normal.

So normal in fact that their new Umayyad overlords, residing in distant Damascus, struggled to get their new subjects to abandon their age-old Zoroastrian festivals, and in the end themselves abandoned the attempt. Moreover, while the early Arab conquerors demanded submission, they did not require conversion. This was in part a consequence of the fact that Islam at this stage was regarded as principally an Arab religion, and perhaps more importantly the realization among the Arabs that conversion was depriving them of much needed and appreciated taxation and tribute. All this, along with the practicalities of the conquest and the realities of geography, meant that in vast tracts of Iranshahr, life pretty much continued as before.

Things would change with the Abbasid revolution in the middle of the 8th century AD and the overthrow of the Umayyads. Contemporary Iranians, and certainly those with a greater interest in an Islamic narrative of descent, distinct from that proffered by the *Shahnameh*, regard the Abbasid revolution, inspired and led, as they understand it, by Iranian converts in Khorasan (eastern Iran), as the beginning of an Iranian awakening. However one seeks to interpret this 'awakening', it is in essence the redrawing of a national myth of descent cloaked in the legitimacy of the new faith. Wherever one might draw the boundary of the ancient inheritance, it is the ability of the Iranians to synthesize the old and the new and to produce something altogether better that is the central achievement of this Iranian awakening, to say nothing of the fact that with the Abbasids, Islam ceases to be an 'Arab' religion, and in Iranian hands becomes a universal one.

There are no doubt parts of this narrative that can be disputed—Khorasan was an area of Arab settlement after the conquest and the Abbasids were undeniably an Arab dynasty—but there is also little doubt that the Abbasids, in moving the centre of gravity of the caliphate from Damascus to the new city of Baghdad, not far from the old Sasanian imperial capital of Ctesiphon, reorientated the caliphate towards the Iranian world. Indeed, as Iranians would point out, the name of the new city was a compound word derived from middle Persian meaning 'given by God'—*bagh-dad.*

Whatever the 'ethnic' provenance of the Khorasani troops who initiated the uprising against the Umayyads—and such distinctions may not be altogether relevant to the 8th century AD—it is probably more accurate to see the revolt as one initiated by the disenfranchised periphery against the centre, and since Iranians tended to be on the periphery during the Umayyad period, it is not difficult to see a coincidence of interests. But it was very much a revolt of one type of Muslim—recent converts—against another type of Muslim, those well-established consumers of conquest and the power that came with it. Of course, and perhaps not coincidentally, just as Kaveh raised the banner of revolt against the despot and placed the rightful king on the throne, so too Abu Muslim, the Iranian Muslim leader of the Khorasani revolt, saw to it that the Umayyad despots were replaced by the legitimate caliphs drawn from the household of the Prophet. A right to rule through blood and kinship outweighed legitimate right through election or selection and some have taken this to reflect the Iranian affection for hereditary monarchy. We shall turn to this in more detail when we look at

Shi'ism and the later Iranian adherence to the minority branch in Islam, but for now the triumph of the Abbasids made explicit a hitherto latent trend towards nostalgia for the Sasanian and a revival of all things Iranian.

The key to this was the bureaucracy. Al Jahiz (d. 868/9 AD), the Arab satirist and commentator, drew the following highly revealing pen picture of the new 'Persian' bureaucrats that had come to dominate the Abbasid administration (trans. adapted from C. Pellat):

> From the moment that he puts on a long full-bottomed robe and takes to wearing his side-whiskers braided on his cheeks and his hair pulled over his forehead in a V, he imagines himself the master and not the underling…Once your novice has sat down…arranged a wicker screen to separate himself [from the common herd] and placed his inkstand in front of him, once he knows by heart the more spectacular clichés…and has learnt the maxims of Bozorgmehr, the testament of Ardashir, the epistles of Abd al Hamid and the *adab* of Ibn al-Muqaffa, and taken the Book of Mazdak as the fountainhead of his learning, and the *Kalila wa Dimna* collection as the secret treasury of wisdom, he sees himself…(as the embodiment of wisdom and learning on earth). His first task is to attack the composition of the Koran and denounce its inconsistencies. Next he demonstrates his brilliance by controverting the historical facts transmitted by tradition and impugning the traditionists…(and he will interrupt conversation about Muslim scholars) to speak of the policies of Ardashir Papagan, the administration of Anushiravan, and the admirable way the country was run under the Sasanians…Among books, the only he approves of is [Aristotle's Logic]…No scribe has ever been known to take the Koran as his bedside reading…If by any chance you come across one quoting passages from the Koran or the *sunna*, his jaws seems to stick as he utters the words, and his saliva does not flow smoothly. Should one of them choose to devote himself to *hadith* research…his colleagues find him tiresome and perverted.

This remarkable passage, albeit intended as a caricature, nonetheless draws attention to some extraordinary realities. In the first place, it may strike some contemporary Muslims as extraordinary that some 150 years after the conquest, there existed a bureaucratic elite that not only drew its inspiration from its pre-Islamic inheritance, but had few qualms in dismissing the intellectual, administrative, or indeed religious competence of the Islamic state at the apparent height of its powers. Indeed, if the pulpit had replaced the throne, it was served by a uniquely Persian civil service, which tolerated the disruption in political continuity rather than admired it. These bureaucrats—broadly defined—were the conveyors of Iranian culture and for all the political instability that was to follow with the rise and fall of competing dynasts, there remained a distinct and remarkably durable Persian bureaucratic thread which ran through the entire history of the Islamic period, extending this 'best practice' far beyond the traditional boundaries of Iranshahr to much of the Islamic world, most obviously India.

What these bureaucrats brought was an intellectual vitality, a disdain for dogma and perceived inefficiency; an adherence to the ideal of administrative excellence and a passion for learning which, later thinkers would argue, betrayed traces—at times quite strong—of what we might now describe as a tradition of humanism. The Abbasids themselves made good use of their Persian bureaucrats, reorganizing the caliphate along more centralized Persian lines and adopting much of Sasanian court practice. A number of caliphs, born of Persian mothers, leaned towards the Iranian territories of the caliphate much to the frustration of their Arab subjects, and adopted the manners and attitudes of their Sasanian forebears, with Khosrow Anushiravan providing the model for a succession of caliphs.

Politics and administration aside, the ubiquity of the bureaucrats ensured that not only culture but language survived. Ibn Muqaffa, noted in the passage above, was one prominent Persian bureaucrat who supervised the translation of many Middle Persian texts into Arabic and afterwards into New Persian—emerging in the 9th century AD, written now in the Arabic script, but retaining its Indo-European grammar and a good deal of its original vocabulary, even if now enriched with Arabic loanwords. There continues to be vigorous debate among scholars about the relative extent of linguistic cross-fertilization but it is becoming increasingly clear that the direction of travel was bilateral and that the contribution of the particular languages reflected both bureaucratic influence and importance of particular fields. So the Arabic language uses more Persian loanwords relating to politics than, for example, theology, though even here, the word for religion—*din*—would appear to enjoy both a Persian and Arabic/Semitic etymology.

Indeed one of the striking aspects of the Iranian renaissance during the mid- to late Abbasid caliphate is the re-emergence of the Persian language, now written in an adapted Arabic script, not as a minority language, which it had been during the high tide of the various Iranian empires—but as the lingua franca of the eastern Islamic world. In this respect the Islamic oecumene did for the Persian language what none of the *Persian* empires could do; it internationalized a language that no longer had a distinct political association. Not only did New Persian—the language of the western Iranian world—come to supersede all other Iranian languages—it became a powerful vehicle for the dissemination of both Iranian culture and Iranian Islam. The Islam that Iranians had helped transform into a universal faith open to non-Arabs was effectively carried to the East on the wings of a distinctly Persian vocabulary.

Quite how and why New Persian became so prevalent is a matter of some debate among scholars especially when one considers that in other parts of the Islamic empire Arabic soon dominated and, for instance in Egypt, a country with a similarly ancient pedigree, effectively replaced the indigenous language. Part of it can be explained through a cultural confidence reflected through the bureaucracy. Some is no doubt a consequence of the size and nature of the conquest itself, which was both sporadic and dependent on local accommodation with regional lords. Although some have argued that Middle Persian was suppressed by the Arabs, the truth of the matter is that it never had achieved the status of a lingua franca, still less a literary language, until it re-emerged as *New* Persian some two centuries after the conquest. Its survival and later widespread adoption may have reflected its relative simplicity compared to Arabic but also its ubiquity among merchants and other artisans who would spread the language along trade routes. The adoption of the Arabic script was far from a constraint on the language and arguably facilitated its use; nor, as some modern nationalists have suggested, was it a radical departure from previous scripts, which were also written from right to left and had the disadvantage of not having sufficient letters. (There is some evidence now emerging that New Persian was first written down in Hebrew letters). In time it was adopted and promoted by a number of successor dynasties in the eastern periphery of the caliphate. What is clear, however, is that Persian never entirely disappeared; it simply adapted—highly effectively as it happened—to new circumstances, and, along with Arabic, it became one of the two 'official' languages of the Islamic world.

As Iranians are only too keen to point out, much of the intellectual vitality of the period was shaped by Iranians, who may have published their main scientific treatises in Arabic—the Latin of the Islamic world—but who also retained an affection for their mother tongue. Ibn Sina (Avicenna, in the West), perhaps the most prolific polymath of the Classical Islamic world, produced works in both Persian and Arabic, dealing with topics as diverse as philosophy and medicine. His 'Canon' served as the medical textbook for European physicians till at least the end of the 15th century AD. But while probably the most famous, Ibn Sina represents the tip of a very impressive iceberg of intellectual talent that came of age in this period: Biruni (d. 1048), for example, calculated the circumference of the globe to within 17km of its true figure, and some 500 years before scientists in the West were able to correctly calculate the figure; Khwarazmi (d. 850) developed algebra; while Farabi's (d. 950) philosophical works earned him the title of the 'second teacher', after Aristotle.

These scholars generally appear, much to the irritation of Iranians today, under the rubric of 'Arab scientists'. It is certainly a matter of contention whether they identified themselves with any particular culture or ethnicity—like good intellectuals they would have no doubt sought to rise above such petty distinctions—but in many cases, their writings do tend to betray an identification with a world view and inheritance that was Iranian in the broadest sense of the term, with the use of idioms, metaphors, and historical examples that reflect an inheritance that was either unconsciously, or more likely consciously, used. This was clearly more obvious among those works that dealt with history (Ferdowsi (d. 1034) of course produced a vast poetic rendition of this history but there were a number of prose accounts), literature, and philosophy, and many of these scientists had occasion to write historical treatises, guides for princes, as well as, in some notable cases, poetry. Omar Khayyam (d. 1092), made famous through the somewhat loose translation of his *Rubaiyyat* by Edward Fitzgerald, was first and foremost a mathematician, who, in echoes of Biruni's achievement, is popularly credited with calculating the solar year to an accuracy not achieved until the availability of precise scientific equipment in the 20th century. This reform of the calendar provided the basis for the Iranian solar calendar to this day. His poetry meanwhile makes both explicit and implicit reference to the Iranian milieu in which he lived with a cynicism towards religious dogma and authority that echoed that of the Persian bureaucrat caricatured above.

The full force re-emergence of the Persian language, the increase in literary productions detailing the history and myths of the

Iranians, as well as the enormous influence of Iranians in administration and their extensive contribution to science in this period, all tend to belie the notion of the Islamic conquest as catastrophic for the Iranians. Iran as a political entity seemed to have disappeared, and existed instead as a literary device and as part of a wider imagination. Yet the political demise of 'Iran' seemed paradoxically to strengthen Iranian culture, releasing it from the bonds of political association to become universal—a similar cultural and literary effervescence seems to have also followed the later Mongol conquest. Some have even argued that Islam liberated Iranian culture, but if so it was a liberation that was fought for from within. Iranians had been conquered before and had ultimately absorbed their conquerors. This one was however different; the break was not only radical, it seemed permanent, forged by a cultural dialogue that was perhaps more bilateral than either side would like to acknowledge. Yet the political break was undoubtedly softened by the reality of a distinct cultural continuity, and it was this continuity that perhaps helps explain the permanence that in time became accepted and part of the fabric of the idea of Iran.

Iran and Turan

The 14th century North African scholar Ibn Khaldun, commenting on the intellectual life of the Muslim world, noted that:

> It is a remarkable fact that, with few exceptions, most Muslim scholars both in the religious and intellectual sciences have been non-Arabs. When the scholar is of Arab origin, he is non-Arab in language and upbringing and has non-Arab teachers. This is so in spite of the fact that Islam is an Arabic religion and its founder was an Arab...thus the founders of grammar were Sibawayh and after him, al-Farisi and Az-Zajjaj. All of them were of non Arab (Persian) descent...they invented rules of (grammar)...Most of the hadith scholars who preserved traditions for the Muslims also were non Arabs (Persians), or Persian in language and upbringing, because the

56

discipline was widely cultivated in Iraq and the regions beyond... all the scholars who worked in the science of principles of jurisprudence were non-Arabs (Persians), as is well known. The same applies to the speculative theologians and to most Quran commentators. Only the non-Arabs (Persians) engaged in the task of preserving knowledge and writing systematic scholarly works. Thus the truth of the statement of the prophet becomes apparent, 'If scholarship hung suspended at the highest parts of heaven the Persians would (reach it and) take it'... The intellectual sciences were also the preserve of the Persians, left alone by the Arabs, who did not cultivate them... as was the case with all crafts... This situation continued in the cities as long as the Persians and Persian countries, Iraq, Khorasan and Transoxiana (modern Central Asia), retained their sedentary culture. But when those cities fell into ruins sedentary culture, which God has devised for the attainment of sciences and crafts, disappeared from them. Along with it, scholarship altogether disappeared from the non Arabs (Persians) who were (now) engulfed by the desert attitude. (trans. F. Rosenthal)

Ibn Khaldun's reflection is unsurprisingly widely quoted by Iranians eager to show just how central they were to the intellectual life of the Islamic world. Few reach the conclusion, where Ibn Khaldun laments that since the depredation of the nomads and the devastation of 'sedentary culture', this situation no longer exists. Ibn Khaldun's observation was a commentary on the impact of the Mongol and subsequent Turkic invasions of Timur on the socio-economic fabric of Iranshahr. If our erstwhile Persian bureaucrat was distressed at the poor administration during the caliphate this was as nothing to the transformation that would take place in the 13th and 14th centuries.

Nomads had been part of Iranian culture since the mythical age when Central Asian Turanians clashed with the Iranians of the plateau. The notion that the lifeblood of Iran needed an occasional injection of raw energy from the Central Asian steppes was not an uncommon theme in Iranian literature. Even the Parthians were occasionally described in such terms. In the Islamic period the Turanians were increasingly identified with the Turkic peoples of Central Asia, who spoke a distinct language but performed the valuable service of providing the military manpower for the Abbasid caliph. These 'slave soldiers' unsurprisingly grew increasingly powerful and as the centre weakened the periphery grew more restless.

By the 10th and 11th centuries successor states were emerging in the East, most obviously the Samanids, who acknowledged the authority of the caliph while pursuing a distinctly Persian cultural agenda. It was the Samanids for example who commissioned the great poetic rendition of the history of the Iranians that would become the *Shahnameh* (see Figure 7). But such was the length of the work that by the time Ferdowsi came to submit it, for his much anticipated reward, the political character of the eastern caliphate had become decidedly Turkic, in the shape of Mahmoud of Ghazna. Perhaps in a reflection of the culture clash to come, Mahmoud proved to be considerably less generous than Ferdowsi had anticipated. As much as he seems to have appreciated the work itself, he seemed less inclined to pay what Ferdowsi considered it was worth and the poet made sure that Mahmoud was repaid in kind in verse.

This tension between urbane sedentary 'Iran' and vulgar nomadic 'Turan' was very real, and even if the latter tended to coerce the former, it was the duty of the former to educate the latter. Perhaps the best example of this tension working constructively was the relationship between the Seljuk Sultan Malik Shah, and his Persian vizier, Nizam al Mulk. The Turkic Seljuks had entered Iran in the 11th century, ostensibly as orthodox Muslim saviours of a dilapidated caliphate racked by both military and religious secession. Not only was the might of the caliphate increasingly restricted to Mesopotamia but the rise of a rival—Shi'a—caliphate in Egypt, along with more heterodox dynasts on the Iranian plateau itself, seemed to signal the imminent demise of the

7. A page from one of many *Shahnameh* manuscripts

'universal' caliphate (Al Andalus in the Iberian peninsula had already seceded some time earlier, but these challenges were far more immediate and dangerous). The Seljuks therefore entered the Islamic world as its protectors and defenders. They came as recent converts and, as they established their authority over much of Iranshahr and Anatolia, they also effectively came under the tutelage of their Persian bureaucrats. Tutelage is a deliberate term. Recent research indicates that Nizam al Mulk took a haughty attitude towards his sultan, and had a manner that did not always endear him. It may ultimately have been his undoing, but before his demise Nizam al Mulk, through his effective administration and the collation of his thoughts in the archetypal Islamic 'Mirror for Princes', his *Siyasat-nameh*—or Book of Government—which draws on both Iranian and Islamic examples to show how best to administer, govern, and regulate the realm, left a profound bureaucratic and intellectual legacy. So popular a manual of government did this become in the Iranian world that it remained essential reading for bureaucrats till the 19th century and is still taught today.

But if the Persianized Seljuks were to prove relatively benign then what followed was of an altogether different scale of ferocity. In the 13th century Iran was witness to two Mongol invasions, the first of which, led by Chinggis Khan, was so ferocious as to lay waste to vast tracts of eastern Iran, and devastate cities that would never recover. Although the scale of the Mongol 'hordes' was undoubtedly exaggerated, the psychological impact of the invasion was palpable in the successive writing of Persian bureaucrats turned historians who could not quite believe the scale of the violence that had been visited upon their kinsmen. This first invasion, largely punitive, was following some 30 years later in 1256 by a more sedate, if far-reaching invasion as Chinggis Khan's grandson Hulegu Khan proceeded to take hold of his 'patrimony', consolidate his grip on the periphery, and crush the centre in the form of the last Abbasid caliph. In 1258 Hulegu sacked the once glorious caliphal capital Baghdad, a city whose religious significance now far outweighed its political importance as the powers of the caliph had long since waned.

Confronted with the hapless caliph, Hulegu took soundings from his advisers, one of whom was the latest Persian bureaucrat cum polymath, Nasir al Din Tusi, whose astronomical observations were to achieve lasting fame. Hulegu enquired whether it was true that if he executed the caliph terrible repercussions would follow. True to his profession, Tusi proved remarkably sanguine about the prospects for upheaval, simply noting that other caliphs had been killed with no serious consequences. As a precaution—since the Mongols remained superstitious about the shedding of royal blood—the caliph was wrapped in a carpet and slowly beaten to death under the hooves of horses. No blood was apparently shed, the caliph died, and Tusi's prophetic accuracy won him a powerful new patron. This tale lies at the heart of a popular Persian metaphor—*namad-mali*—common in describing relations of all sorts, to describe the idea of pushing and provoking just as far as you think possible—without shedding blood or going so far as to incur an unwelcome reaction.

Hulegu came to rule and to found a new dynasty—the Il-Khanids—and if the new rulers had little interest in the welfare of their subjects, they wanted to ensure that there was some wealth to extract. In order to do this as efficiently as possible, they needed administrators, and true to form the Persian bureaucracy swung into action behind their new overlords, although it would be fair to say that educating them was to prove a good deal more difficult than their predecessors. One notable vizier, who became governor of Baghdad, and who wrote a history of the early conquest, Ata Malik Juvaini, lamented the drop in educational standards and the subversion of social norms that accompanied the Mongols, along with the upsurge in superstition and millenarianism that often results from such a political, social, and psychological trauma. In one memorable passage reminiscent of the tradition of Persian bureaucratic condescension, Juvaini noted that 'They consider the Uighur language and script to be the height of knowledge and learning.' Still, by the turn of the 14th century the Mongols had converted—albeit by all accounts reluctantly—to Islam, and, in an extraordinary process of cultural absorption, effectively (sub)merged into their environment—a process that was in marked contrast to their experience in China where they were expelled by force of arms.

The impact of the Mongol Conquest could have been considerably ameliorated by a prolonged period of recovery and reconstruction but the lull of the 14th century did not last long and within two generations Iran was subject to the arguably more vicious depredations of Timur—known in the West as Tamerlane—whose ambitions to outshine the Mongols in brutality compounded the damage and ensured the permanence of the changes in the political economy of the country that had taken place. Timur centred his imperial ambitions on Samarqand, and for him Iran was simply an accessible source of loot. It is estimated that he launched some seven invasions of the country, repeatedly plundering the resources and preventing any serious economic recovery. Although the Mongols are largely blamed in the Iranian popular consciousness for the destruction of Iranshahr, and by some accounts, are the source of Iran's continued 'backwardness' in terms of general global economic and political development, it is probably also true that the depredations of Timur set the seal on this transformation.

So what was this change? In the first place, as Ibn Khaldun noted, the invasions altered the fundamental political economy of the country by effectively transforming it from a sedentary agrarian economy sustained by a wide network of irrigation channels, to one that was essentially pastoral and nomadic. The Mongols had no time for either cities or irrigation; what they were interested in was pasture. These pastures existed increasingly in the north-east and north-west of the country with the result that the southern areas—the Persian heartlands—were neglected. The focus of power shifted from the south and west to the north. Mesopotamia, the heart of Iranshahr and the seat of the imperial capitals of Babylon, Ctesiphon, and Baghdad, went into terminal decline, dependent as it was on the maintenance of extensive irrigation. The political elite were now more distant than ever to their subjects. The Seljuks were Turkic but they were heavily Persianized and had already converted to Islam. The Mongols, and to a lesser extent the Timurids (who had converted), were interested in, but not awed by, the culture they had conquered. For them the Chinggisid inheritance was all-important. Moreover, for all their lack of interest in religion, the one thing they did contribute was the Turkic language, which now dominated, in vast swathes of the pastoral lands in the north, in a way that Arabic never did.

But there were more subtle ways in which the integration between Iran and the new Turanians would take place, with interesting if unforeseen consequences for the future. First, and perhaps most interesting, was the enthusiasm which the Mongols and their Turkic successors showed for the *Shahnameh* and their association with Turan. Indeed the Turkic dynasties that followed were far keener promoters of the culture of the *Shahnameh* than the 'Iranians' that immediately preceded them—the earliest extant *Shahnameh* manuscripts we have date from the Mongol period. The myths of the *Shahnameh*, which drew to a great extent on the nomadic culture of the Central Asian steppes, enjoyed an immediate appeal that could only be enhanced by its lack of religious proselytizing. It enjoined a chivalric code that the warriors of the steppe could relate to. In this rather curious way, the Turkic warriors who had caused such devastation to the Iranian world actually bought into the Iranian ideal and became active promoters of it. Another means of dissemination was inadvertent—the migration of bureaucrats and intellectuals fleeing the onslaught to both India and Anatolia. It was these migrations that can be said to have laid the foundations for the Persianization of the emerging Ottoman and Mughal administration, along with the further spread of the Persian language, at the same time as Turkic languages were making such an impact upon Iran proper.

Indeed political catastrophe had the paradoxical effect of encouraging a cultural and literary renaissance with an increase in prose histories and arguably the apogee of Classical Persian poetry through the works of Saadi (c.1210–1291)—the great ethical poet of the Persian-speaking world—and Hafiz (c.1326–1390)—the great mystic, courted by Timur, and celebrated centuries later by Goethe. Saadi's admonishment to kings that 'The children of Adam are of one essence', and do not deserve to be called human if they are indifferent to the pain of others, stands as a testament to the profound humanism of Iranian thought and is now engraved at the entrance of the UN building in New York.

It is perhaps a reflection of this curious cultural turn that the concept of Iran, as a political term, returned during this period. Having abolished the caliphate, the Mongols effectively facilitated the rebirth of Iran-Shahr, now redefined for the new age as Iran-zamin—the land of Iran.

Shi'ism

Some modern discussions of Iranian identity—especially those emanating from the political establishment in Iran today—place Shi'a Islam and its myths and rituals at the core of that identity. It is a position that is actively promoted by the revolutionary government though its reception through society is probably less enthusiastic than it was in the heyday of revolution. Shi'ism in a sociological, if not necessarily theological, sense remains a key component of that multi-layered entity known as Iranian identity, in part of course because Iranian Shi'ism—like Christianity in the West—was most successful where it reinforced spiritual and religious beliefs that already existed. Given its prominence today it is easy to forget that for the better part of a millennium from the time of the first Muslim conquest, Iran was, in elite terms at least, a bastion of Sunni orthodoxy—though this statement itself requires some qualification.

Divisions within the Muslim community are traditionally traced to the dispute which arose over the succession to the Prophet

Muhammad, with the Sunni traditionalist majority arguing that the succession fell to the best individual who was selected from the community—essentially from the Prophet's inner circle. This has often been described as the elective principle, though given the context and time, selective might be a better descriptor. Shi'as, or the Party of Ali, as the name suggests, argue that in actual fact the Prophet had decreed that his successor should be Ali, his cousin and son-in-law, and that the leadership of the Muslim community devolved upon him and his heirs—thus a hereditary succession. In the event Ali was passed up for the succession and only eventually took over the leadership as the fourth of the Rightly Guided Caliphs. His rule is held up by Shi'as as the epitome of just government and a weighty tome of sage rulings and wise counsel is ascribed to him and forms a central pillar of Shi'a theology and learning. Ali was, however, undone by the schisms and political conflict which racked early Islam, and he was eventually murdered while at prayer. It is difficult to underestimate the role of Ali for religious Iranians, and among the more devout he is the fount of political wisdom as well as the gate to religious knowledge.

His sons Hasan and Hussein sought to challenge for the leadership against the emerging Umayyad dynasty (based in Damascus), with each taking a different approach to the political realities of the day. Hasan chose to concede political power to the Umayyads, recognizing that a challenge would be futile. He has been, as a consequence, largely unfavourably compared to his younger brother Hussein, who decided to challenge for the leadership. With a small band of followers (traditionally 72), he set out to confront the usurpers, was ambushed, and slaughtered on the plains of Karbala. His selfless martyrdom in pursuit of justice became the touchstone of Shi'a theology and it is not difficult to see how this particular political myth appealed to Iranians inured—through the *Shahnameh*—to the concept of justice and the tragedy entailed in its pursuit against the odds. It helped that in time it was suggested that Hussein had in fact married one of the daughters of the last Sasanian king, Yazdegerd

III (632–51), thereby fulfilling the hereditary principle from two legitimate sources: yet another example of Iranian accommodation and adaptation.

Despite the best attempts of modern Iranian scholars of Shi'a history, there is little evidence of distinct schools of thought in the Muslim community till around the 10th century AD, still less of any particular inclination among Iranians towards this minority view, outside perhaps a sympathy for the rebel with an apparently just cause. Indeed, Shi'ism, insofar as it did enjoy adherents in the Iranian world, probably did so because it resonated with a general sympathy for heterodoxy and the 'resistance' it seemed to provide against the authority of the day. At the same time, the development of Shi'ism as a distinct doctrine and epistemology held attraction for an intellectual elite that wanted to be at once Muslim but different, and sought a theology that resonated with their own often eclectic religious inheritance. Moreover the esotericism created a dichotomy between the inner (*batin*) and outer or explicit (*zahir*) that had valuable practical uses in allowing one to disguise beliefs in the face of potential repression. It could at best provide theological justification for political resistance and, at worst, legitimize mendacity.

But on a purely theological level Shi'ism offered intriguing possibilities, offering both the esoteric mysticism of a spiritual saviour through the personage of the imam, in this case Ali (the first imam) and his descendants, along with a comparatively rigorous and rational approach to the pursuit of knowledge through the application of reason. Put simply, and this is a simplification, while the various Sunni schools were wedded to the authority of the day and combined legalism with a profound reliance on faith, Shi'ism responded with a much more speculative and inquisitive theology that searched for the truth, and argued for a continuous interpretation of scripture according to context and time. Ultimate authority lay with the imams, who enjoyed the final word on any (re-)interpretation. But the important point was that the living imam's rulings could supersede those of his predecessors. This principle of continuous interpretation was of particular relevance to the appreciation and understanding of the Quran. Was it a timeless miracle, the word of God for all ages; or could it only be understood in the context of its time?

Such views, which had originated in mainstream Sunni theology, were subsequently, through systematic repression, relegated to and adopted by the minority Shi'a school of thought. They had also largely developed in the febrile intellectual environment that was Mesopotamia, which, as noted above, in the early centuries of Islam, retained much of its Sasanian inheritance and character. On the Iranian plateau itself these more heterodox views naturally found greater resonance and resilience in territories far from the centres of authority, most obviously in the mountainous north and the Caspian littoral. Yet Shi'ism did not first achieve political power in Iran but in North Africa under the Fatimids, who subsequently established their power base in Egypt. The Fatimids claimed descent from Imam Ali through the Seventh Imam (whom they considered the last, hence their appellation of Sevener Shi'as).

A further schismatic branch—the Nizari Ismailis—emerged in northern Iran under the leadership of one Hasan al Sabbah, who effectively operated a state within the Seljuk sultanate through a network of mountain castles that only eventually succumbed to the Mongols, some two centuries after their foundation. Hasan al Sabbah is regarded by some modern Iranian nationalists as an Iranian patriot resisting the oppression of the Seljuks, though aside from the fact that the political network he established was in part sustained by a sympathetic local population, it is difficult, and indeed anachronistic, to portray him as some sort of proto-nationalist. Indeed, the Nizari Ismailis, known colloquially as Hashashin, because of their apparent fondness for hashish—a term that was subsequently Latinized into 'assassin'—grew increasingly unpopular with the authorities because of their success in murdering key opponents, such that the Mongols were positively welcomed when they successfully eliminated them as a political threat.

The Mongols themselves were not particularly interested in the nuances of religious theology, and for all that they eventually came to publicly espouse Sunni orthodoxy, the religious environment they oversaw remained febrile and heterodox. This partly reflected the folk religion that accompanied the nomadic culture that the Mongols brought in their wake. Indeed there was a good deal of difference between theory and practice as far as the Sunnism of the Mongols was concerned, given its incorporation of parts of the shamanistic and folkloric elements of their own traditional religious beliefs. But the trauma of the conquests (and those of Timur that followed) also created a crisis of instability that lent itself to a host of eclectic, esoteric, and charismatic movements. Juvaini, for example, recounted one rebellion in Khorasan—that of Mahmud the sieve-maker—with particular disdain, noting his claim to be in communication with spirits and to be able to cure blindness, miraculous powers that led Juvaini to the following droll observation: '...if I should see such things with my own eyes, I should concern myself with the treatment of my eyesight.' The political and economic turmoil lent itself to millenarianism, and, for all its rationalism, Shi'ism was uniquely equipped to respond.

As has been already noted, knowledge and spiritual leadership in the Shi'a community was the prerogative of the imams. But this depended on a continuous hereditary succession. The Ismailis considered that the legitimate succession ended with the seventh imam, but the larger branch of the Shi'as considers that the succession extended to the twelfth. A crisis in leadership became manifest when the succession failed, as it did with the accession of the Twelfth Imam. Since the Twelfth Imam had succeeded to the leadership of the community at a very young age, he remained hidden for his own protection. This period was known as the Lesser Occultation. After a period of some 70 years it was agreed that he might not actually reveal himself and had instead disappeared into another dimension, hidden from the real world as the sun might cloak itself in clouds, only to reveal himself at the end of time and the worst of times, to restore justice and universal peace. The Twelfth Imam—Mahdi—henceforth the Hidden Imam, had thus entered into Greater Occultation.

It is important to bear in mind that occultation meant that the imam was present but not visible, and one of the immediate problems for the Shi'a community was how to articulate this reality, and thus maintain the cohesion and continuity of the community, without facilitating the theological turmoil that might result from individuals claiming to be in communion with him. One way was to indicate that the Hidden Imam had pointed out that anyone making such a claim was either a liar or a madman. The other was to develop a rigorous intellectual hierarchy to effectively protect access to this esoteric canon of knowledge. The rationalism of Shi'a epistemology was therefore cultivated and nurtured by a growing class of learned men, or clerics, who sought to define and delimit access to, and the parameters of, this particularly powerful religious knowledge. They, and the rationalism they promoted, often sat uneasily with those divines and mystics who claimed some spontaneous and charismatic connection with the knowledge and power projected by the Hidden Imam. Thus over time Shi'ism facilitated another duality between rationalism and superstition, the tension between which also came to shape Iranian attitudes towards religion and political power. In the social and economic turmoil that accompanied the Mongol and Timurid invasions, the esoteric utopia of the mystic often trumped the dour rationalism of the intellectual.

Power accrued to those who could in time combine this religious charisma with practical acumen. In the late 15th century, one mystical Sufi order in particular, the Safavids, came to prominence in north-western Iran and, under the leadership of the boy prince

Ismail, seized power over much of the Iranian heartlands and, for a brief moment, eastern Anatolia. The source of Safavid power, located as it was in the north-west and dependent on Turkic tribal religious warriors, known as the Qizilbash (red-heads, on account of their head-dress), reflected in part the changes in the geography of power left by the Mongol invasion. They also, in their mystical and millenarian aspirations, were a product of the political turmoil of the post-Mongol period. Shah Ismail entered Iranian history at the tender age of 12 when he conquered Tabriz, around 1501. He achieved this feat in no small measure because his soldier-acolytes believed him to be an expression of the divine, and for some—including probably Ismail himself—to actually *be* divine. Claiming descent from the Shi'a imams—a genealogy their enemies would challenge—somewhere along the line, this Sunni Sufi order became avowed Shi'as, but not, given Ismail's self-identification, a Shi'ism that would have been familiar to the orthodox. Ismail's Shi'ism was most definitely of a heterodox and millenarian kind, and, given the devotion of his followers, it helped him conquer an empire. Had the Ottomans not defeated him at Chaldiran in 1514, he might have succeeded in adding much of the Anatolian plateau to his Iranian lands.

Ismail proved sufficiently charismatic to survive this particularly decisive defeat—he was reported to have been consoled only by copious quantities of drink—but for the better part of a century afterwards the Safavid state was on the strategic defensive, if never under serious threat of being overwhelmed. The situation changed with the accession in 1587 of Shah Abbas, known to posterity as 'the Great', and the only monarch of the Islamic period to have been viewed with a mixture of awe and affection by his people. If Khosrow Anushiravan is popularly held to have constructed every pre-Islamic monument, then Shah Abbas is credited with almost everything worthy from the Islamic period. His architectural legacy is certainly impressive, especially in the city he made his capital, Isfahan, which he adorned with magnificent buildings worthy of the craftsmanship of the era, most strikingly the Shah Mosque which occupies one side of the central square (renamed after 1979 as the Imam Mosque).

Shah Abbas confirmed and institutionalized the political rebalancing of the Safavid state, away from the exclusivity of the earlier period towards a more inclusive and pluralistic structure that drew on all the talents of the imperial mosaic that made up the state, while focusing attention on the central authority of the king. This was the 'King of Kings' in the traditional Iranian sense, as Leviathan. The tribal Qizilbash were reined in; a military paid from the central treasury was established and an administration run by erstwhile Persian bureaucrats rationalized the taxation system and accrued money from customs and trade. In reconfiguring the state Shah Abbas was able to go on the offensive and for a brief period the boundaries of Iranshahr (or -zamin by this stage), including Mesopotamia, were united in one political state. Success at home was reflected in victory abroad, which rebounded to reinforce the king's majesty at home. It was a virtuous circle, and in the eyes of his contemporaries, including a growing number from the West, Shah Abbas could rightfully claim his place among the Renaissance princes of the day.

Continuity and change

Shah Abbas's legacy would prove to be a powerful one and serves to reflect the cumulative inheritance of the preceding generations. His ability to combine and harness these to his own political will was the secret of his success and his successors were never quite able to fill his shoes. But it says much of his achievement that the century or so following his death has been characterized by some historians as one of protracted decay and decline on account of the general peace that was experienced. Shah Abbas above all was able to reconcile Iran and Turan within the state; the Turkic and the Persian, the nomadic warrior with the sedentary bureaucrat. The new Turkic layer represented the distinct Chinggisid inheritance that had brought in its wake a wave of Turkic tribesmen. The Safavids themselves, whatever their ethnic origin, were always more comfortable speaking a form of Turkish within their households, with Persian reserved for government and administration. Yet as the new Turan they were an integral part of that whole that was Iranian civilization, and the Safavids were likewise at ease with this distinctly Iranian inheritance (the Safavids are among the very few post-conquest dynasties to have drawn inspiration from the *Shahnameh* for throne names), which they promoted as a part of a strategy of cultural superiority against otherwise dangerous rivals in the form of the Ottomans to the West and the Mughals to the East.

The greatest distinction of the Safavids from previous rulers in Iran, and the one that is most misunderstood, is their promotion of Shi'ism. Until 1501, Iran had been regarded as a bastion of Sunni Islam. The Mongol conquest made explicit a heterodoxy that was never too far from the surface, and the febrile religious environment that emerged was to be ultimately exploited by the Safavids. The Safavids effectively transferred their allegiance from a heterodox form of Sunnism to an equivalent form of Shi'ism. Their lack of adherence to any form of orthodoxy probably made this transition all the more smooth and explicable. Similar to their Sasanian predecessors, whom posterity has also characterized as zealous promoters of their faith, the Safavids were far more eclectic, inclusive, and pluralistic in their approach to religions than popularly recognized. Shah Abbas himself began his life as a pious prince but ended it more of a cynic than many of his religious admirers might be willing to accept. In contrast Safavid Shi'ism began eclectically and ended riven with dogma and ritual, as later diffident, indolent, and pious kings facilitated and encouraged the growth of the learned *ulema*, the clerics who would in time both reinforce and ultimately undermine the authority of the monarch.

With organized religion becoming part of the fabric of the state as it had been under the Sasanians, so too did a clerical class, beholden to the state and servants to that state, emerge in force. Their influence was not only seen in the gradual conversion of the country to Shi'ism but in the massive injection of religious terms—largely Arabic—into the language, such that with the previous importation of Turkic, Persian became a truly cosmopolitan language. It is a remarkable fact that it is easier for a contemporary Persian speaker to read the 10th century Persian of Ferdowsi than the complex vernacular that emerged from the Safavid experience. This complex imperial mosaic might flourish under dynamic leadership, but its absence would result in centrifugal forces that would ultimately consume it.

Chapter 4
Iran and the West

Commenting on the influence of Shah Abbas the Great, the
Huguenot merchant Sir John Chardin, long resident in Isfahan
in the latter half of the 17th century, noted that, 'When this
strong and noble prince ceased to live, Persia ceased to prosper.'
Chardin's assessment has been reflected in subsequent analyses
that have argued for a long slow process of decline arguably
precipitated by the very policies of administrative centralization
that Shah Abbas had instituted. The consolidation of authority
could only work when the political will of the ruling monarch
was active, energetic, and ever present. An indolent and/or
decadent monarch, who paid little attention to the realities of
government, would inevitably facilitate administrative decay
and corruption.

This assessment of course also reflected the prejudices of the
Protestant Chardin whose notions of decline and its causes were
not only informed by his religious leanings but arguably by his
experiences of the absolute Catholic monarchy of Louis XIV.
Indeed Chardin's commentary, widely quoted following the
publication of his bestselling 'Journey to Persia', provided the
template for a distinctly Western narrative understanding of Iran
which presented the decline of the East (in this case Persia) as a
context for the rise of the West.

This narrative arc has been painstakingly constructed over time and is both uni-linear and increasingly Eurocentric in its understanding of *progress*. Not only has it shaped a Western idea of the decline of the East but it has also impacted Iranian understanding of their own predicament. Indeed the impact of the West on Iran and the Iranians has been both material and, in much more subtle and interesting ways, intellectual. For better or worse, the logic of the West has been pervasive, and it is to this final influence on the identity and character of Iran that we must now turn.

Decline, fall, and salvation

Chardin's presence in Iran in the latter half of the 17th century reflected a new turn of events, as Western merchants increasingly began to make their presence felt in the East (see Figure 8). Hitherto, the West for Iranians meant Rum (Rome): Greeks, Romans, Byzantines, and latterly Ottomans. These represented the near abroad of the Iranian world, both familiar yet distinct. In the 16th and 17th centuries, the West in the Iranian imagination began to expand westwards as increasing contacts were made with the rulers beyond the traditional frontiers of Rum, who were eager to secure both economic opportunities and political advantage with Iran against the Ottomans. Shah Abbas was perhaps the first Iranian monarch to systematically treat with the West in the form of merchants, missionaries, and ambassadors who travelled to his capital at Isfahan. Political advantage proved difficult to come by, or at least to coordinate, but trade in goods and ideas grew with a good deal of the direction of travel from Iran to the West. So dominant has the narrative of decline become that it is often forgotten that in the 17th century Europeans went to Iran as supplicants rather than conquerors and that the balance of power very much lay with the Iranians. Few relationships express the change more clearly than Iran's relations with and attitude to the Russians—then known as Muscovites—who occupied a humiliatingly low status in the diplomatic pecking order. Indeed

8. Europeans in Iran, from the *Chehel Sotoon* Palace in Isfahan, 17th century

in the 17th century it was the Russians who were the 'barbarians' and the Iranians 'civilized', and few Europeans would have argued differently. Within a century these positions would have effectively been reversed; not, it should be emphasized, in the Iranian appreciation of themselves, but certainly in the appreciation of Iranians by others. For Iranians, this dramatic change in their international circumstance proved a particularly bitter pill to swallow.

The pivotal period for this transition was the 18th century. As Europe embarked on an Enlightenment and scientific revolution, Iran entered a period of prolonged political and economic turmoil. This singular distinction is important for understanding the nature of the decline and its impact upon the popular consciousness in Iran. Far from being a slow process of political decay whose roots could be sourced to the reforms of Shah Abbas, the collapse of the Safavid state was much more precipitous, and even European observers were shocked at the rapidity of events. That they then retrospectively explained the collapse in terms of protracted decadence—a view that was not entirely alien to Iranian observers—should not disguise the reality that most contemporaries did not think that dissolution was imminent.

Much as with its Sasanian predecessor, the collapse of Safavid Iran resulted from an unfortunate conjunction of events confronting a divided political class under an indecisive monarch. In this case trouble came from the east in the form of rebellious Afghan tribesmen. Dispatching forces to suppress the uprising, the Safavid Shah, Sultan Hussein, who had discovered an unusual level of piety even for his kinsmen, decided, for reasons that remain unclear, not to continue to supply his forces. They were subsequently defeated and the Afghan rebels moved westwards and discovered that the Safavid government was unusually inept in resisting their advance. It was not that they could not put forces into the field—though peace for the better part of 100 years had blunted the military effectiveness of the Safavid state—but leadership was divided and coordination woeful. The result was that the Afghans found themselves at the gates of the imperial capital Isfahan, and after a prolonged and devastating siege, during which time famine consumed much of the population, the hapless monarch surrendered to his former subjects with the pitiful comment that God had clearly decided that Mahmud, the Afghan warlord, should succeed to the throne. Few were more surprised by this turn of events than Mahmud himself.

But perhaps what is more striking is not so much the precipitous fall, but the dramatic salvation that followed. If the Afghans were not the zealots of the Arab Muslim conquest—they sought to inherit rather than overthrow—the collapse of the Safavid state was, much like that of the Sasanians, more of a personal and dynastic failure, than one of the state itself. The Safavids enjoyed a continued religious authority among the populace that would stand putative successors in good stead, and which the Sasanians did not have, but as before, the conquerors came to absorb and benefit from the administrative system they found. Mahmud himself proved to be among the least successful of the 'barbarians' to seek to dominate the Iranian state, soon becoming intoxicated with his success and adopting the worst possible characteristics of the decadence that had facilitated his victory. If the destruction wrought by the Mongols and their successors was to enter popular history as the source of the many ills that had befallen Iran, they were still admired for the 'noble' savagery and martial qualities they possessed. The Afghans, as peoples that were considered Iranians, albeit poor cousins, were henceforth to be tainted with the brutality and vulgarity of Mahmud. However unwarranted it may be to generalize from the depravity of one man, it is a condescension that Iranians hold towards Afghans to this day.

Mahmud's brutality engendered resistance from outlying parts of the state far sooner than many had anticipated, but the success and revitalization that was to follow—almost as dramatic a rise as the fall that had preceded it—had much to do with the political and military genius of one man, Nader Afshar—a warlord in the service of the Safavid heir apparent, Tahmasp—who was able to use the extant powers of the Safavid state to remove the Afghans. Nader proved remarkably successful in his reconquest of Iran. Soon after the Afghans were expelled he drove the Ottomans from their new acquisitions in western Iran and negotiated a Russian withdrawal from the Caspian provinces they had opportunistically annexed. Increasingly contemptuous of the Safavid prince on whose behalf he was ostensibly fighting, Nader determined to usurp the throne for himself. In 1736, after a decade of war, Nader succeeded in crowning himself king of a new Afsharid dynasty.

He then proceeded to expand his realm in new directions, with a dramatic descent on Delhi in 1739 that dealt a fatal blow to the Mughal dynasty. He returned to Iran with an unprecedented hoard of gems and jewellery including the fabled peacock throne. These successes unfortunately, though not unprecedentedly, resulted in a mixture of hubris and paranoia which in turn—after the blinding of his son in a fit of jealousy—led to melancholia and cynical depression. The continued cycle of wars that had exhausted the country both politically and economically, combined with Nader Shah's erratic behaviour, convinced his subordinates that the king was detrimental to the peace of the state, and they resolved to assassinate him. Nader's end proved as ignominious and precipitous as his rise had been sudden and dramatic. Far from bringing peace, his lieutenants fought over the spoils of empire.

If Nader Shah's fall reinforced the narrative of decline, his meteoric rise had forced many to reconsider. His conquest of Delhi brought him to the attention of international observers who hailed him as the new Alexander. At the height of his powers, his rule was pregnant with promise for the future, not only in terms of his militarization of the state and the implications this might hold for a military revolution, but in his ambitions, aspirations, and attitude towards power. Nader Shah was the first king to envisage the construction of a navy for the Persian Gulf, to project Iranian power to the southern littoral of the Gulf, and to protect against the intrusions of European maritime powers. He had a particular idea about the authority of the monarch and was disdainful of what he thought was the overweening and interfering power of the clerical classes. Indeed his treatment of the Shi'a *ulema*, now themselves liberated from any state control and allegiance to the Safavid dynasty, would have been familiar to many a secularizing monarch in the West.

In seeking to have Shi'ism included as a school of Sunni orthodoxy, Nader has been accused of being both expedient and naive. But that he could broach this at all reflected an awkward reality that the sources of his legitimacy were Iran and Turan, not Islam. Coins struck for the occasion of his coronation noted emphatically that he was 'Nader of Iran-zamin, and world conquering Khosrow'. Unsurprisingly, the clerical classes were to prove unforgiving. His brutality has normally been held against him but Nader's behaviour was not much different from that of

Peter the Great, who had gone one further and actually murdered his son. What was signally different, however, was that Peter had taken the first steps towards the institutionalization of the state away from the person of the monarch. Nader never began this process with the consequence that when he died, his very personal empire collapsed with him.

For Iranians today, the lessons of this period are distinct and different from that which might have been learnt by a European observer. Politics remained personal and leadership was paramount. A popular if apocryphal tale relates that Nader Shah was campaigning in the mountains of Afghanistan when he caught sight of an elderly man fighting with considerable vigour nearby. Impressed, he asked him where he was when the Afghans were busy ravaging the country. To which the old man retorted, 'I was here but you were not.' In the absence of leadership nothing works: the great many are nothing without the will of the great man. And the will of the great man can set things right in a relative instant. In the absence of central authority there is instability and unpredictability. Order can only be restored by a skilled and ruthless leader. Disorder is much worse than tyranny and much is forgiven a ruthless ruler if at least he can restore order. For many Iranians today, Nader's military successes are justification in themselves and more than outweigh any brutalities that accompanied them.

The experience reinforced a tradition to seek salvation in (strong) leaders, and to treat power as personal and fragile. The belief that nothing lasts and that the wheel of fortune may soon turn on the whim of powers over which you have no control reinforced a fatalism born of religious belief and cemented through experience. In time, a religious belief in the cycle of despair and salvation would translate into a political belief, in which the role of unseen power would be played by the emergent imperial powers of the West. Religious superstition thus became political superstition and the conspiracy theories of the present. This period of turmoil and the febrile and anxious atmosphere it engendered echoed sentiments that followed the Mongol onslaught and, like that period, the recovery was prolonged even if the challenges to be posed by the rising European powers were of a wholly different nature.

Although Nader Shah's fall inaugurated another period of political turmoil there was still a conviction that, as with Nader himself, salvation would be round the corner. In the first instance this took the shape of a division of the spoils between Nader Shah's generals, one of whom established the framework of modern Afghanistan, while one of Nader Shah's grandsons established himself in Khorasan, and another former lieutenant, Karim Khan Zand, took control of the west. Karim Khan is a remarkable figure in Iranian history in part because he did not seek the title Shah, seeing himself instead as the representative (*vakil*), a term which some have taken to mean that he had populist if not democratic leanings. It may well have meant that Karim Khan did not consider a dynastic claim to be legitimate and that he was still paying lip-service to the Safavids. Of one thing we can be sure, Karim Khan mended relations with the Shi'a *ulema*, and indeed the clerical hierarchy, who, in the absence of a Safavid state, had effectively created their own 'state within a state' and now operated with far more independence than had hitherto been possible. There is little doubt that their gratitude helped mould Karim Khan's subsequent reputation, since he was not averse to the use of violence when it was required. At the same time, Karim Khan's rule benefited in the public eye from the fact that it represented a relative political lull between the blood and fury of Nader Shah and the next dynastic challenger to enter the scene.

Agha Mohammad Khan Qajar must qualify as one of the most remarkable if brutal dynastic founders in Iranian memory—and given his proximity to the present day, that memory is remarkably fresh. A scion of the Qajar confederacy (the word tribe does not do justice), the Qajars traced their origins to one of the Turkic tribes that had entered Iran with the Mongols and then had served as one of the warrior clans under the Safavids. They were convinced that they were the true heirs of the Safavids and that Nader Shah had usurped their inheritance. Both his father and grandfather had been defeated in their challenges for the throne, and 'Agha' Mohammad Khan, a title given to him on account of the misfortune that befell him, was castrated at the age of 6 by one of his rivals ('agha' signifying the fact that he was a eunuch), in lieu of an execution.

Taken in by Karim Khan, where he lived at the court under house arrest, Agha Mohammad eventually escaped to mount his challenge for control of Iran. One can only imagine what sort of impression this beardless pretender to the throne made on those he sought to bring round by persuasion and coercion. Especially when one considers that his voice will not have broken. Suffice it to say that Agha Mohammad Khan's guile and brutality impressed some and horrified many, and learning the lessons, as he saw it, of Nader Shah's failure, he determined to eliminate everyone and anyone who might pose a challenge to the stability of the dynasty. Sir John Malcolm, one of the first British emissaries to the court of Qajars, commented ruefully that Agha Mohammad Khan was the price Iran had to pay to end nearly a century of political turmoil and that the targeted terror was a necessary evil to restore the authority of the monarchy. In truth, Agha Mohammad Khan was, on the whole, more calculated than reckless in his use of violence. His premature death—he was murdered in his bed in 1797—was followed by the smooth succession that he had fought for all his life, facilitated by bureaucrats who had grown tired of the continued instability and welcomed by a populace exhausted by war. Iran had nonetheless paid an exceptionally heavy price for the political settlement that saw the authority of the king re-established in a political consensus centred on the Qajar extended family intermarried with the landed aristocracy, and supported by a clerical hierarchy anxious to consolidate the faith and a merchant class eager to make money. This social and religious base was further enhanced by Agha Mohammad Khan's embrace of a distinctly Iranian narrative of kingship, founded on the ideals of the *Shahnameh* (which he would have recited to encourage his troops into battle), and expressed with the invention of a 'Kayanid' crown. Indeed, when Agha Mohammad Khan 'accepted' the crown with the words that he intended to be among the greatest kings of Iran, his dynastic horizon undoubtedly lay far beyond the Safavids.

Enlightenment, civilization, and barbarism

In 1848, while much of Europe was engulfed in a wave of revolution, Iran was in the grip of a revolution of its own, as a series of uprisings in favour of the 'Bab' (the 'gate') began to rock the religious and subsequently political settlement of the Qajar state. It was probably the most serious challenge to the stability of the Qajar state and monarchy until the Constitutional Revolution in 1906, but its religious and millenarian character has resulted in it being interpreted as a hangover from an earlier age rather than a harbinger of change. The Babi Revolt nonetheless tells us much about Iranian state and society in this period, and both it, and the reactions it elicited, were pregnant with consequences for the future.

Agha Mohammad Khan's settlement was predicated in part on an explicit agreement with the Shi'a clerical hierarchy, in which they would support the legitimacy of the dynasty in return for protection. This Shi'a 'church' was neither as organized nor as disciplined in a theological sense as some might retrospectively argue. The hierarchy was by no means as formalized as it is today and in theological terms there was considerable scope for various sects and mystical groups to emerge, relating to the esoteric qualities of religious knowledge and one's relationship to the Hidden Imam. As noted above, the febrile religious environment was similar to that which had existed in the centuries after the Mongol conquest.

One group, known as the *Shaykhis*, grew increasingly popular in the first half of the 19th century. They cultivated a belief in the imminent return of the Hidden Imam. Before he died in 1843, their leader counselled his followers to seek out his successor, who in 1844 was declared to be the 24-year-old Seyyed Muhammad Ali, from a mercantile family in Shiraz, who had since an early age eschewed commerce in favour of religious meditation. His extreme piety, though reportedly distressing to his parents who would have far preferred him to stick with the family trade, won him followers from among the Shaykhis and beyond, and his importance to his followers grew so that by 1848 he declared himself to be the Hidden Imam returned. As shocking as this undoubtedly appeared to orthodox Shi'as, what was striking about this revelation was the apparent inclusivity of the whole project. Reminiscent of the universalism of Mani in the Sasanian empire, the Bab presented himself as the saviour promised not only in Muslim tradition, but also in biblical and Zoroastrian tradition. He was seeking to merge and extend the Abrahamic and Zoroastrian traditions, the religious traditions of ancient and modern Iran.

The authorities were remarkably sanguine about the Bab until his claims grew so dramatic that they were persuaded to act. But interestingly, when the Bab was first arrested and put on trial the judgement came down that he was simply deluded. It was only his subsequent claim that he was the Hidden Imam, the Mahdi, that qualitatively altered the situation, since one of the consequences of the return of the Hidden Imam was the effective suspension of all religious law. This obviously had political consequences and the authorities were forced to detain the Bab, while his followers launched a nationwide uprising to get him released and to proclaim the new age. At last the authorities moved to crush the uprising, and the Bab himself was executed with further widespread and brutal pogroms to follow. Ultimately, one of the Bab's followers, Bahaullah, reformulated the faith on a pacifistic platform and migrated abroad to spread what would become known as the Baha'i faith.

The Babi Revolt shook the traditional pillars of Shi'ism and forced a consolidation and clarification of theological principles as well as of the hierarchy, to prevent a repetition of such millenarianism. The obsession with which the traditional hierarchy have sought to eliminate the Babi and subsequently Baha'i 'heresy' is testament not only to the external threat Babism posed, but also to continued anxieties about internal dissension. Babism and the millenarianism it espoused are regularly denounced as 'foreign' heresies, but the truth of the matter is that it emerged from within the body of early 19th century Shi'ism, and its emphasis on a saviour and the myth of salvation is, as has been shown, a recurring theme in Iranian history.

For Iranian intellectuals struggling with the political problems of the day and most obviously the challenge posed by Western imperialism, the Babi experience provided contradictory lessons. The mere fact that, in the full light of history, an individual could declare himself the messiah and acquire a significant following was a source of major embarrassment to intellectuals who had begun to sup at the table of the European Enlightenment. For them, this was an expression of the very superstition they sought to eradicate from the Iranian body politic, even if some of the ideas that had emerged from the Babi challenge to orthodoxy, especially in relation to education, were remarkably enlightened for their day. Yet they were equally horrified at the brutal pogroms that had followed. This was worse than superstition; it was barbarism, and it drew the opprobrium of a West that had since seized the moral high ground.

The Iranian encounter with Europe and European civilization had begun in the Safavid era, but it only became systematic in a political sense from the early 19th century. In the earlier period attempts to reach a political alliance against the Ottomans had faltered in part because of the limits of early modern communication and the difficulties of coordinating policy. The emphasis had lain in commerce and culture. But in the 18th century political and cultural developments, including the emergent Enlightenment, had ensured that East and West had begun to move along diverse trajectories such that the admiration of the 17th century gave way to contempt. The military revolution, the dominance of the rule of the law, along with distinct ideas about crime and punishment, all began to distinguish a European civilization which no longer drew inspiration from the Orient. If in the 17th century the logic of civilization looked east, in the 19th century—following the onset of the Enlightenment—the logic had moved emphatically westwards.

Napoleon's invasion of Egypt in 1798 along with the steady march of Russian forces south through the Caucasus and Central Asia alerted both the Ottomans and the Iranians to the challenges of European power and their inability to respond. Although the Europeans, as noted above, tended to cultivate a narrative of Oriental decline, to correspond with their own rise, for the Iranians, their military and political weakness in the face of Russian aggrandizement was all the more galling not only because they'd traditionally viewed the Russians with some contempt, but also because of the dramatic nature of their fall from grace. Only fifty years earlier, the Russians thought better of challenging Nader Shah in the field, and the latter had sent commissioners to oversee the withdrawal of Russian forces from the Iranian provinces of the Caspian littoral.

Now Agha Mohammad Khan confided to his prime minister that he would not risk a direct confrontation with Russian forces but would instead employ a scorched earth policy. When his nephew and successor, Fath Ali Shah, did confront the Russians, he was badly defeated and humiliated in two wars that saw Iran lose its Caucasian territories, principally Georgia, Armenia, and the territory that now composes the Republic of Azerbaijan. These losses were acutely felt—the Treaties of Golestan (1813) and Turkmenchai (1828) are regularly cited to this day as examples of deep national humiliation—and attempts to seek recompense in the east by securing control of Herat were foiled by Britain, anxious to protect its possessions in India with the establishment of Afghanistan as a buffer state. Indeed with the Russians to the north and British India to the south and east, Iran found itself vulnerable to two rising powers (if one looks at India rather than the British empire in India) it had traditionally viewed with some disdain. Moreover, unlike previous challenges, these new powers were no longer seduced by the charms of Persian civilization but came bearing a civilizing mission of their own.

All this ensured an unprecedented crisis of identity, which served to undermine the cultural self-confidence that had till then characterized Iranian attitudes to the outside world. In this sense the challenge of the 'European' Enlightenment was similar to that posed by the Muslim Arabs in the 7th century. Yet if the Arabs came bearing a new faith, the manner and nature of the conquest, to say nothing of the slow pace of conversion, gave the Iranians both time and space to adapt as well as to be convinced. In this case, the challenge was sudden, and comprehensive. The Europeans might continue to be susceptible to conversion to key aspects of Iranian arts, literature, and culture, but Persian government, politics, and religion, those areas in which Iranians traditionally felt superior, no longer held much attraction, beyond historical curiosity.

The response was nonetheless perhaps more nuanced than modern critics would admit. If Iranian civilization found itself on the back foot, this in itself was not unprecedented and the approach tended once again towards a negotiation through areas of perceived common ground. In this case, despite the ideological challenge being faced, the very cosmopolitanism of an Enlightenment that had yet to become definitely 'European' facilitated the negotiation. Indeed, the ideas about the acquisition of civilization and manners, the rule of law, the distinction between superstition and religion, and the importance of a rational education, were not entirely alien to the bureaucratic-intellectual traditions of Iran. It was the manner of their application that was different: the dominance of the rule of law, the institutionalization of government away from the personality of the sovereign, and the development of an education that was 'scientific', in the broadest understanding of that term.

There was enough that was familiar to make adoption acceptable and desirable, and the argument that was made was that European *civilization* was simply an extension and development of those ideas acquired from and lost by the East. The areas of extension—the innovations of this particular enlightenment—related to the institutionalization of the rule of law and the development of the idea of individual rights in the context of the growing power of the state. Iran and the Iranians could therefore reclaim their rightful place among civilized peoples (increasingly defined in the political discourse of the day as 'races' or 'nations') by reacquainting themselves with these values. Only then could the tendency towards barbarism and savagery—tendencies that might afflict all civilizations that had lost their way—be contained and the promise of (Iranian) civilization be fulfilled.

There are few better examples of the complexity of this dialogue with the West than the relationship between Jamal al Din al Afghani and his Western interlocutors. Despite his adopted surname, Afghani was a product of the febrile religious and intellectual environment of 19th century Iran, and scholars have suggested he adopted the moniker to disguise his Shi'a roots. In Iran today they have taken to calling him by the town of his birth—Asadabadi—in an obvious attempt to reclaim him for the resurgent national narrative. Afghani acquired both a dislike of the dogma and superstition of this religious upbringing as well as—following a sojourn in India—a profound suspicion of European imperialism. Focusing on the latter, his traditional followers throughout the Middle East (he enjoys a very strong intellectual following in the Arab world) regard Afghani as an advocate of a reinvigorated (political) Islam overturning European imperialism. Yet Afghani never rejected the fundamental ideals of the Enlightenment, frequently engaged with, and was admired by, European intellectuals, and arguably regarded the shortcoming of personal monarchy and the dogma of orthodox religion as the true causes of Oriental decline.

In a memorable exchange (published in the French *Journal des débats*) with the French philosopher Ernest Renan, rarely cited and often denied by his more devout supporters, Afghani concluded with his reflection on the relationship between religion and philosophy, dogma and enlightenment:

Religions by whatever names they are called, all resemble each other. No agreement and no reconciliation are possible between these religions and philosophy. Religion imposes on man its faith and its belief, whereas philosophy frees him of it totally or in part. When the Christian religion...entered Athens and Alexandria, which were, as everyone knows, the two principal centres of science and philosophy, after becoming solidly established in these two cities its first concern was to put aside real science and philosophy, trying to stifle both under the bushes of theological discussions, to explain the inexplicable mysteries of the Trinity, the Incarnation and, Transubstantiation. It will always be thus. Whenever religion will have the upper hand, it will eliminate philosophy; and the contrary happens when it is philosophy that reigns as sovereign mistress. So long as humanity exists, the struggle will not cease between dogma and free investigation, between religion and philosophy; a desperate struggle in which, I fear, the triumph will not be for free investigation, because the masses dislike reason...and because, also, science, however beautiful it is, does not completely satisfy humanity, which thirsts for the ideal and which likes to exist in dark and distant regions that the philosophers and scholars can neither perceive nor explore. (trans. N. Keddie)

The humanism—and cynicism—of the Persian bureaucrat was alive and well. The struggle between enlightenment and dogma, civilization and barbarism, Iran and Turan, continued, and the challenge for Iranians was to negotiate a new settlement, albeit with terms defined increasingly by others. This negotiation was made easier by the explicit cosmopolitanism of the early Enlightenment and the obvious debt it expressed to Oriental ideas, manners, and civilization: a civilization that the Enlightenment had repackaged for the industrial age and now sought to re-export. The fact that many of the themes seemed so familiar made Iran's engagement with the challenge of the West more intimate, nuanced, and profound than many could have imagined.

Revolutions and reform(ation)

Few concepts exemplify the logic of the West more clearly than the adoption of the ideas of the 'nation' and 'revolution'. If the concept of identity and Iranian-ness was not as 'modern' as some have argued, the systematic re-conceptualization of that term along with the ideological means to socialize and popularize it, through an ideology of *nationalism*, was quite new. Indeed the 'modern' age brought with it a zeal for categorization and definition that denied ambiguity and forced upon Iranians a clarity of choice that was disquieting. No longer would it be possible to obfuscate and demur in the margins. The new 'science' of politics encouraged clarity not only of thought but increasingly of identity—one really had to know who one was before one could even begin to know others. The politics of identity suddenly became—as a consequence in part of mass education—ideological and exact. The application of these ideas in terms of both definition and popularization reflects the real revolutionary change that has been taking place.

Sir John Malcolm had reflected in his study of Iran that few nations had undergone so many revolutions as Iran and yet had remained so unchanged. For him, living in the aftermath of the French Revolution, it was remarkable how the political turmoil of

18th century Iran had effectively restored the *status quo ante bellum*. What changed in the 19th century and the revolutions that followed was the injection of ideas—most potently that of 'progress'—harnessed and disseminated through technological change. The industrial revolution transformed the political landscape, enhancing power, (re-)enforcing it, but also, in the information revolution that would follow, liberating it from the centre, creating centrifugal forces that were increasingly efficient in resisting the growing power of centralized government. This was a new periphery at the heart of the state; an increasingly educated society empowered by technology. These new dynamics would affect the way in which the idea of Iran and Iranian identity would be constructed and understood with new challenges and renewed attempts to navigate an inclusive middle ground.

A tale of two revolutions

It is a common conceit of the present to consider events that are proximate to our own time to be more important and of greater consequence than those that are more distant and less immediately familiar. The tendency is to revisit the past in order to explain the present, but this teleological fallacy results in the accentuation of some trends at the expense of others, and in the absence of a broader historical context within which to situate these trends, we are often left with a picture that is both less accurate and less focused than would be useful for a rounded understanding.

The proximity of the Islamic Revolution both in terms of time, and through the wonders of modern mass communication, and in terms of space—it was perhaps the world's first televised revolution—has ensured that for many, this revolution remains the seminal event of modern Iran, and, because of its effects on the United States, one of the turning points of the late 20th century. Political revolutions are, by definition, surprises, and, unsurprisingly, political analysts and historians rushed to explain why they had not foreseen it. What they had missed was not insignificant, but, perhaps by way of intellectual penance, there was a tendency to over-interpret an Islamic inheritance that was always part but never the totality of Iranian identity. Not only was this Islamic inheritance more seamlessly integrated into the narrative than was historically realistic, it was also enthusiastically promoted by a clerical class that was unusually united in both its views and direction of travel. This tendency to re-view history through the prism of the Islamic present was of course nothing new but it was not in time to go unchallenged, and unlike previous governments the Islamic Republic faced a population that was both more educated, connected, and interested in their past.

The first great revolution to profoundly affect the Iranian political landscape was the Constitutional Revolution of 1906. This revolution, a product of nearly a century of engagement with Europe and the ideas of the Enlightenment, profoundly altered the political and social direction of the country and laid the foundations for much that was to follow. Its main tenets, if yet to be realized in practice, have become such an integral part of the political and ideological fabric of the country that few people can imagine the situation beforehand, or indeed a political settlement that did not include the idea of parliamentary democracy, the rule of law, mass education, and, perhaps most importantly, constitutional limitations on power.

That these ideas exerted a powerful influence on Iranian politics, and, by extension, the politics of identity, was in large measure the consequence of the adoption and adaptation of the ideas of the Enlightenment to an Iranian context by a number of leading Iranian intellectuals, the vast majority of whom had become members of Masonic lodges, where they had been welcomed as part of an international intellectual fraternity. The enthusiasm with which Iranian intellectuals—including Jamal al Din al Afghani—became Freemasons is indicative not only of the cosmopolitan nature of the early Enlightenment, but of the means by which these ideas became embedded. The vague Masonic affectation for Zoroastrian imagery, the rituals of membership, the emphasis on rational thought and condemnation of superstition, and the need to believe in an omnipotent deity—though not the Trinity—all made Masonic membership not only attractive but relatively easy for Iranian intellectuals. For many, the Masons represented an acceptance by, and a return to, an all too familiar universal tradition of humanism: a return to civilization and its values.

Central to their ambition for translating their Iranian Republic of Letters into a Republic of Laws was on the one hand the development of constitutional—legal—government, with a separation of powers and a unitary sovereign authority—the Shah—limited by laws. In this, they absorbed the observations of a number of European travellers to Iran, who had argued (as noted in the Introduction) that the great inhibitor to progress was not the Iranians themselves but the haphazard and arbitrary nature of their government, which encouraged instability. The Shah might serve to maintain harmony in the imperial mosaic, but too much depended on the competence of the individual shah, and the Qajar dynasty seemed uniquely capable of producing uninspiring monarchs. The absence of royal salvation and the mounting challenge of Europe convinced Iranian intellectuals that some more drastic measure might be required. Appalled by what appeared to them to be the degeneration of Iranian state and society reflected in the humiliating defeat in foreign wars, brutality at home in the treatment of Babis, and a rank inability to maintain themselves as a second-rate, let alone first-rate power, Iranian intellectuals became increasingly convinced that what was needed was durable institutional change to ensure stability and provide the necessary platform for development. This demanded constitutional changes that limited the power of the monarch and instituted the rule of law.

Development was not understood in raw political or economic terms, but fundamentally in social and educational terms. If the prerequisite for development was good governance, then the goal was to achieve better Iranians through a broad education and an awareness of the self. For the first time, identity, and what it meant to be an Iranian, would become a matter of state policy. What had hitherto been a preoccupation of the elites and the princes they sought to educate now became a necessity for the general population. Good governance could ultimately only be sustained by the widespread cultivation of virtuous citizens. The project was still heavily elitist but the ambition was democratic.

These matters initially came to a head in 1906, when a coalition of intellectuals and progressive clerics allied with members of the bazaar challenged the authority of the Shah and demanded the establishment of constitutional government complete with a representative parliament. Modelled on the Belgian and ultimately the English Constitution, the new Iranian constitution, much lauded by British intellectuals and roundly dismissed by tsarist Russia, was not only ahead of its time, it was also well beyond the comprehension of most of the people it was intended to serve. Enthusiastic deputies elected in some haste and without proper preparation to the first Parliament (Majlis) were quick to launch a legislative programme for the construction of a modern state complete with universal education. They were less eager to find ways to finance this impressive programme of reforms, and the initial enthusiasm soon gave way to infighting as the coalition fragmented in waves of recrimination about the meaning of constitutionalism and the revolutionary project that accompanied it.

Three distinct splits began to emerge: the first and most important was over the desirability of a constitution at all. The supporters of constitutionalism won this argument, even if disagreements remained about the detail. That this principle was won at all was to prove a significant achievement because henceforth the idea of constitutionalism would be an important political point of reference. The nature of this adherence became an important factor in subsequent disagreements over the style of the constitution and how in particular its religious and secular components should relate to each other; but finally, and perhaps most importantly in light of recent history, the relative balance between the rights of the state and those of its citizens: in short the balance of the social contract to be imposed.

Many of the leading intellectuals of this period were forced to concede that priority must be given to the construction of the institutions of government since the early constitutional experience had taught them that ambitions were irrelevant in the absence of the tools of government required to implement them. The emphasis, in the decades following the Constitutional Revolution, was on the development of the state, and a considerable amount was achieved, which ultimately facilitated an exponential growth in education, symbolized in 1934 with the foundation of the University of Tehran. Education was the linchpin of the social project at hand, and it is to this and the defining and cultivation of Iranian identity that we must now turn.

Education and identity

A modern state could no longer be sustained and developed by a reclusive and restrictive elite; it could only be sustained by the cultivation of an educated and stake-holding citizenry. This was to be an idea of Iran for and with the participation of Iranians. In short, Iran's intellectual elites recognized their time-honoured duty to 'educate their masters', but their masters were changing.

One of the leading intellectuals tasked with defining an idea of Iran and Iranian identity for the modern era of mass consumption and intellectual democratization was Mohammad Ali Foroughi (see Figure 9). Foroughi was the scion of a traditional bureaucratic family who had studied law and been pivotal in the development of a School of Law of Political Science in Tehran at the turn of the 20th century. Foroughi, like many of his politically active intellectual contemporaries, was a Freemason who had absorbed

9. Mohammad Ali Foroughi

the ideas of the Enlightenment. For him, History and Identity
were intimately intertwined and no 'civilized' people could exist
without a history. Rejecting the racial theories of the nation that
were beginning to dominate in a number of European countries,

Foroughi argued that Iranian identity was founded on a shared history and language, and this language was emphatically Persian. This was not to deny the value of other languages or dialects, but if Iran was to move from an imperial to a national state and to provide for mass education, there had to be a degree of conformity and standardization.

A balance had to be achieved between the centre and the periphery—for far too long had favoured the periphery, and now the state had to emphatically establish its authority. But the doctrine of centralization, which was to dominate nationalist thinking in Iran, had yet to take hold, and the mechanics of power were not yet in such a state of technological advance to facilitate the sort of centralization that might in time suffocate the periphery and provoke local reactions. In the first half of the 20th century neither ideas nor capabilities had reached such a pass, and men like Foroughi argued for a harmonious balance between the centre and the periphery, the state and its citizens.

For citizens to be empowered they had to be educated. And education required a curriculum that was modelled, as in the West, on new disciplines of history, geography, law, and language. History had to be taught as it was, not as it had been imagined. Iranians had to become reacquainted with Cyrus and weaned off their dependence on Jamshid. Yet Foroughi was among the most forceful of his generation to warn against the discarding of the traditional histories and myths, or their relegation to the realms of literature. History and myth both had a role to play in the defining of an Iranian identity for the modern era, for if history provided the people with facts about their past, mythology fed the soul, and provided an inclusive ethical framework for what it *meant* to be Iranian (see Figure 10). Such an approach was all the more important when faced with the rigorous nationalisms of neighbours in Turkey and the Arab world. Turks, Kurds, and 'Persians' could all be part of the universal inclusivity of the *Shahnameh*: the many could indeed become one.

10. Kaveh reimagined, leading the people from 'darkness' to 'light', from the eponymous nationalist newspaper published 1916–22

Foroughi died in 1942 and within a generation his ideas and admonishments had been largely forgotten. The state that he helped create grew increasingly powerful and centralized with little compensation for society, while the civic nationalism and empowered citizenry he envisaged soon found itself increasingly restricted and dictated to by a state whose power had been reinforced by both technology and the growing flow of oil revenue. On the one hand the state was facilitating mass education that encouraged self-awareness and responsibility; on the other, it demanded deference to an elite that was becoming in its turn increasingly repressive. If Foroughi had encouraged a love for the *Shahnameh*, it was not for its kings but for its heroes and for the ethical principles it enshrined which might imbue in Iran's new citizens a sense of personal responsibility and initiative. Yet the relegation of the *Shahnameh* resulted in an increasingly sterile cult of personality formed around new historical and political myths that did little to liberate the individual and much to reinforce a tradition of deference and dependence. On a deeper historical level this revolved around the figure of the great emancipator, Cyrus the Great, reimagined for the contemporary age and most obviously tailored to the demands of the Pahlavi dynasty. Other, lesser historical figures were recruited into service to fulfil an Iranian fascination with the myth of the saviour. In this sense the Enlightenment project espoused by Foroughi had singularly failed.

Thus supporters of the strong state have tended to focus their attention on the two monarchs of the Pahlavi dynasty—Reza Shah (1925–41) and his son Mohammad Reza Shah (1941–79)—for their promotion of political and social change and, in the case of Mohammad Reza Shah, for overseeing the dramatic economic development of the country, while detractors have sought to blame them for all the ills that have befallen the country. Similarly, the noted Nationalist Prime Minister Dr Mohammad Mosaddeq, overthrown in an Anglo-American engineered coup, is regarded by constitutionalists as the paragon of republican virtue, while Ayatollah Khomeini, who eventually came to overthrow the monarchy and establish the Islamic Republic, is regarded by his supporters as the saviour who restored Islam to the heart of Iranian identity.

The Islamic Revolution and the Islamic *Republic* it created are as much children of that first revolution. While some sought to implement the ideals of the Enlightenment and others fought against it, all were ultimately driven and shaped by a vocabulary inherited from it. If Khomeini and the Islamic Revolution sought to identify themselves against the centralizing power of the monarchy the political system he established did little to alter the direction of travel and even reinforced the modern autocracy being created. Reza Shah and Mosaddeq were products of a Constitutional era that ultimately sought unity in diversity. For all their differences, Iranians were part of a whole and enjoyed, by virtue of their citizenship, certain rights. This was reflected in the development of new penal codes and the abolition of torture for political prisoners.

But in the second half of the 20th century, as the state grew more powerful and identity more political and exclusive, torture returned with a vengeance as a means, not only of extracting confessions, but also of breaking an individual. The dignity of the 'citizen' was thus systematically shattered on the altar of ideological expediency driven by the demands of a Cold War that had little to do with the Iranians. It was an ideology that increasingly forced people to choose. Economic and political development empowered the state and the person of Mohammad Reza Shah in ways his own father might have aspired to but never achieved. The centralization of power that ensued contradicted some of the main tenets of the Enlightenment project such that the power of the state overwhelmed the power of the citizen and the Shah increasingly took it upon himself to define and dictate the parameters of what it meant to be Iranian for the modern age. This was the reification of Iran without Iranians. Indeed the real departure from the ideals of the Constitutional Revolution came long before 1979 as Mohammad Reza Shah's identification with Cyrus the Great and his development of the notion of sacral monarchy witnessed the development of a highly personalized and mystical monarchy that sought in time-honoured fashion to mediate between the spiritual and material world.

In this sense the Revolution of 1979 and the imposition of a theocracy was a confirmation and not a rejection of the trends established by Mohammad Reza Shah. Khomeini had won support by appearing inclusive and drawing a broad range of malcontents to him, including socialists and staunch secular nationalists. But on achieving victory, he governed exclusively, disowning those who had brought him to power and defining everything on the basis of a radical and personal interpretation of Shi'a Islam that was rooted in esoteric tradition but exploited all the tools of modernity available. Iranians soon found that Khomeini and his acolytes were no more willing to tolerate an inclusive ambiguity than the Shah had been: identity was to be defined by the state and it was up to individuals to sign up to the new doctrine. As with Mohammad Reza Shah, Iranians themselves were excluded from the idea of Iran.

Politics and society

Yet in one respect the state that was built on the ruins of the monarchy was quite distinct, and that was its peculiar institutionalization of a dual system of government in a constitution for an *Islamic Republic*. This reflected the broad church that unleashed the revolution accepting the reality of a 'republic' drawn from ideas that would have been familiar in 1906. But a parallel theocratic establishment was constructed around the authority of the Guardianship of the (religious) Jurist, ostensibly to protect against the return of autocracy but effectively and practically reinforcing and extending it. One of the main crises of modernity—the debate between autocracy and democracy and its implications for ordinary Iranians—was therefore locked into the new constitution and the supreme Jurist emerged as a new Leviathan to arbitrate a dispute that had now been constitutionally sanctioned. Far from eliminating autocratic rule, the incoherence of the new constitution encouraged a far more personalized form of autocracy, exploiting modern technology and means of government, to reinforce traditional forms of power.

This central contradiction has lain at the heart of the political disputes that have periodically shaken the Islamic Republic but this central tension also represents an unholy marriage that goes some way to explain the durability of a system that thrives on ambiguity. The Islamic Republic, like the Iranians themselves, appears to defy definition. It is at once theocratic and autocratic, yet as a succession of visitors will relate—often with a sense of bewilderment—it seems to be also possessed of democratic characteristics, not simply in the fact that it holds regular elections, but more profoundly in the eccentric, idiosyncratic, and outright rebellious nature of its people. Indeed the paradox at the heart of the contradiction is that while political ambiguity might facilitate autocracy, the sheer inefficiency or arbitrariness of that autocracy also allows society considerable room for manoeuvre. The absence of law is repressive but it also makes it difficult to contravene and provides room for negotiation.

Sometimes that room expands, at other times it will contract. At the beginning of the revolution, the new regime sought inclusivity, but in the turmoil that followed the overthrow of the Shah, it became restrictive and ruthless in the pursuit of the opposition. It was helped at first by the onset of the Iran–Iraq War—perhaps the seminal event in the history of contemporary Iran with social repercussions that are still being felt. As the war became prolonged, Iranians became more demanding, and a transition appeared to be taking place from subjects to citizens; women began to play a far more important role as men departed for the front. Above all the government relaxed its control, eager to keep society onside. The end of the war witnessed a gradual opening of Iranian politics and society, first through economic reform but most dramatically in the surprise election in 1997 of the moderate Mohammad Khatami, a reformist with a keen sense of the Enlightenment project. For Khatami public education mattered and the first few years of his presidency witnessed the most dramatic expansion of the country's press since the Constitutional Revolution in 1906. Universities once again became centres of fierce debate; journalism became the profession of choice for the nation's aspirant youth. For all the limitations of Khatami's political reforms, the intellectual and social changes he unleashed were dramatic and unsurprisingly stung his hard-line opposition into a bitter and violent reaction. Confronted with enemies at home and abroad (9/11 had put an end to Khatami's attempts at détente with the West), his presidency came to an ignominious end in 2005 with the election of Mahmoud Ahmadinejad, a man whose intellectual pretensions sought to mask vulgar demagoguery and populism. Fuelled by high and rising oil prices, Ahmadinejad's bombastic presidency saw society constrained and ambiguity go to the heart of the state. Flush with money, Ahmadinejad could indulge and defer any decisions. It was not only the state that now lacked clarity; even its decision makers seemed bewildered by their own genius, until a dose of economic reality shook them from their stupor.

For society at large it was a case of continuous adaptation to the ambiguous realities of the present. Nothing lasted, everything was negotiable. Art, culture, and politics always sought to push back and the politics of resistance were often subtle, be it in the curiously retractable nature of women's headscarves, or the determination of men to shave and even occasionally wear a tie. This process has had a positive effect on Iranian art (including cinema) which has had to resort to increasingly subtle and ingenious forms of myth and metaphor to get its points across. It occasionally manages to get through the censors, who are much more responsive to visual representations (too much flesh on show) than the deeper messages that might be imparted. But as intriguing as this process of continuous negotiation might be, the continuing uncertainty and instability it engenders grows ever more tiresome and frustrating. What used to be occasional is, in our modern age, more frequent and intrusive as an increasingly powerful state seeks to interfere and 'negotiate' in more aspects of life than ever before; against a society of increasingly educated and self-aware people who seek room for more responsibility.

A crisis of 'modernities'

In his essay on the question of 'What is Enlightenment', Immanuel Kant argued that 'Enlightenment is man's emergence from his self-incurred immaturity. Immaturity is the inability to use one's own understanding without the guidance of another. This immaturity is self-incurred if its cause is not lack of understanding, but lack of resolution and courage to use it without the guidance of another. The motto of enlightenment is therefore: *Sapere aude!* Have courage to use your own understanding!'

No statement perhaps encapsulates more thoroughly the ambitions of a generation of Iranian intellectuals in the first half of the 20th century. Yet within years it became apparent that this ambition was easier in the breach than in the application and Iranians remained wedded to their leaders—political or religious—for guidance and instruction. In part, as Kant would have argued, this was a consequence of indolence or fear of the unknown, but there were also other practical issues of time and context that would have affected the success of a project that, in educational terms at least, would take at least a generation to achieve results.

In other important aspects it was the failure of the politics of the country to respond to the changes taking place in society that obstructed and indeed reversed the educational trends set in place in the first half of the 20th century. Increasingly disempowered at home, Iranians sought redemption and explanation in traditional forms, alternately seeking mysterious and esoteric religious and political explanations for the trials and tribulations of life. In our modern age, those who could not seek refuge in religion turned instead to a new *political* superstition: the conspiracy theory, which found all the ills of the country in the abstract machinations of 'foreign' powers. The West, and to a lesser extent Russia, now joined the Macedonians, Arabs, and Mongols in being blamed for the variety of ills that afflicted Iranian state and society. Given the historical proximity of the European challenge, it was the impact of these powers that loomed large in Iranian politics. It did not help of course that foreign powers had regularly interfered in the politics of the country, but the solution, as Iranian intellectuals argued, was to empower yourself and by extension your country such that foreign powers would no longer dare to interfere, not through the cultivation of a self-defeating paranoia.

Yet if the potential of education was constrained by politics, it was extended by technology, which allowed the inquisitive to negotiate a way out of government control. Mass education combined with mass communication to transform the way in which Iranians viewed themselves, locally and within a global context. Perhaps most strikingly the emergence of a successful Iranian Diaspora after the revolution of 1979 has convinced many of them that their weaknesses are not ingrained but, as those early European observers argued, determined by the nature of their government. Perhaps the clearest indication of this social change occurred not during the presidency of Mohammad Khatami but in its aftermath. The state's determination to crush what it defined as the heresy of reform and the idea of freedom—defined by one cleric as Western idolatry—has met with resistance that has gone far beyond the constant negotiations alluded to above. It is in sum not always society that has pushed the boundaries of the envelope too far. More recently it has been the state that has misjudged the political and social mood of the country, dismissing political sentiments at their peril, as they witnessed to their cost in the election crisis of 2009. Indeed, it says much of the social and educational revolution permeating the country that a decade of push back and repression could not ultimately contain a social movement that remained intellectually vibrant and internationally connected. Mass communication has not always had a rationalizing effect, of course; the worldwide web can both challenge and reinforce convictions, and perhaps unsurprisingly the internet has become the new terrain to be contested and negotiated.

But this is qualitatively different terrain with far-reaching consequences. Iranians, to paraphrase Kant, are not only beginning to think for themselves, they are exploiting new technologies to express these new ideas. Blogging has become the new mode of contestation, with Persian language blogs among the most numerous and active worldwide. As with other media, the state has relented and engaged with it, encouraging its own bloggers to challenge and push back against those who see the medium as the latest means of forcing the political envelope. Yet even these 'authorized' bloggers are escaping control, edging out from the centre to the periphery, and challenging orthodoxies. Iranians are in sum discovering their identity anew, scouring their history, and reclaiming it. Young Iranian Muslims now proudly claim Zoroaster as their first prophet, blithely unaware of the contradiction they have endorsed. Others boast that Cyrus the Great was a prophet. Every Persian new year, Iranians in increasing numbers attend commemorations at the tomb of Cyrus the Great in Pasargadae. These are all developments that have not gone unnoticed by government, but far from refuting them they have sought to exploit the public mood. Ahmadinejad went to great lengths to secure the loan of the Cyrus Cylinder and could barely contain his emotion when it was unveiled in Tehran. A senior member of the religious establishment even went as far as to proclaim Cyrus a progenitor of monotheism, an extraordinary claim for a senior Muslim cleric to make.

Yet just as if not more important than this reclamation of history has been the restoration of the nation's myths to the central position they once enjoyed. As Foroughi once argued, if Cyrus had founded the Iranian monarchy it was Ferdowsi and his compilation of the *Shahnameh* who had revived the Iranian nation. It was this mythology that defined it and elevated it to the highest ranks of civilization. As Mohammad Khatami, perhaps the most popular and socially receptive politician to have been elected to high office in the Islamic Republic, said in a speech he delivered to expatriate Iranians at the United Nations in 1998:

Mythology describes the spirit of various nations. And there is no nation or people whose history is free from myth. Of course, in conformity with the weight of civilization and the history of a nation, the myth of the nation is deeper and more complicated. And civilized nations usually have myths. The ethical myth and the myth epic indicate the spirit of Iranians...the Book of Kings [is] the symbol of Iran.

Chapter 5
Iran and the Iranians

Like all peoples, Iranians are products of their environment, both spatial and temporal. These have been negotiated, interpreted, and contested over time. The sort of continuities that staunch nationalists like to promote do not reflect the complex inheritance that Iranians carry with them, but it is also true that as a political culture and civilization, the idea of Iran and the Iranians has sustained some striking continuities. This can be seen in the persistence of the language, with words that can be rooted and traced into Old Persian. But it is also present in the cultures and habits of those who identify themselves with the Iranian world. It is the very flexibility and adaptability of this culture that makes it durable, and to begin to understand Iran and the Iranians, one has to appreciate the totality of the vision it seeks to reproduce.

Iran is conceived of as a civilization with a distinct creation myth that has survived a series of challenges that would have overwhelmed less assured peoples. It enjoys universalist pretensions that are more than a match for anything that the Christian or liberal West has been able to produce. It sustains a series of apparent contradictions—dialectics if you will—that maintain its vitality, a creative destruction that does not always strike the right balance. It has often fallen short of its own—civilizational—ideals. The roots of this duality lie in Zoroastrian tradition and are reflected in a rich mythology that articulates a struggle between Iran and Turan, the

11. A contemporary Iranian poster, symbolizing the continuing negotiation between myth and history; tradition and modernity; Islam and nationalism

sedentary and the nomad, the centre and the periphery, and more recently religion and nationalism (see Figure 11). It has been enriched and at times empowered by varied challenges from beyond its borders, be they Western, Arab, or Turco-Mongolian.

To begin to understand Iran is to appreciate its history, both real and mythological, to see how different influences have been woven into a complex tapestry and how each layer has reinforced and redirected various traditions. Traditions remain important, and if they are subject to continuous reinvention—not least in our modern technological age—it is remarkable to what extent Iranians will seek refuge from the present in the comfort of an imagined past. So dominant has that past become that it has arguably diminished any confidence in the future. Transcending that tradition and harnessing it for the future has been at the heart of the progressive agenda for a century or longer. There is no doubt a degree of complacency and self-assurance born of the *longue durée*, a confidence in the continuity of the idea of Iran. Over the vicissitudes and vagaries of time, Iran somehow re-emerges. To paraphrase that keen observer of Iran, Lord Curzon, 'History suggests that the [Iranians] will insist upon surviving themselves.'

The Western challenge has been the most intriguing. It is the most recent, and the least acknowledged. But it is also one of the first. The Western powers reminded Iran both of its earlier greatness and of the Greeks and Macedonians who first resisted Iran and then seized its empire. Iran was midwife at the birth of the idea of the 'West'. It was the context against which the West would come to be defined, and to understand the other is, in some way, to better understand ourselves. The early Western Orientalists understood this fundamental fact when they went in search of knowledge in the East. It is perhaps a truth that our modern—boundary ridden and oppositional—world has forgotten. But it is a truth that is implicit in the history, the poetry of Saadi, and in the myths of the *Shahnameh*: We are all born of one essence; we are all the children of Fereidoon.

Chronology

Myth

The Pishdadian dynasty
The Kayanid dynasty

History

BC

5000	Earliest excavated settlements
2700	Rise of Elamite civilization in south-western Iran
2000–1000	Arrival of the Aryan tribes on the Iranian plateau
1200	Zarathustra reforms the religion of the Iranians
800–600	Rise and rule of Median Empire
559	Cyrus the Great and the formation of the Persian Empire
539	Cyrus the Great conquers Babylon
490	Darius the Great attacks Greek mainland
480	Xerxes launches second assault on the Greek mainland
332	Persian Empire conquered by Alexander of Macedon
330–238	Seleucid dynasty in Iran
c.240	Emergence of the Parthian Arsacid dynasty
53	Parthians defeat Crassus at Carrhae

AD

Iran

1946	Azerbaijan Crisis, start of Cold War
1951–3	Oil Nationalization Crisis
1953	Coup orchestrated by MI6/CIA overthrows nationalist Prime Minister, Dr Mohammad Mosaddeq
1979	Islamic Revolution overthrows monarchy and establishes Islamic Republic; seizure of US Embassy on 4 November
1980–8	Iraq invades Iran; Iran–Iraq War
1989	Death of Ayatollah Khomeini; Ayatollah Khamenei becomes Supreme Leader
1989–97	President of Ali Akbar Hashemi Rafsanjani
1997–2005	Presidency of Mohammad Khatami
2005–13	Presidency of Mahmoud Ahmadinejad
2013	Election of Hasan Rouhani

Chronology

Further reading

There are a number of general reference texts available for those interested in investigating the subject in more detail. The most comprehensive history is provided by the seven volumes of the *Cambridge History of Iran*, the first volume of which was published in 1968. While some parts clearly do not reflect the latest research, as a set, it still holds up well. A new and increasingly valuable resource is the steadily expanding *Encyclopaedia Iranica Online*, which provides detailed articles on an extensive range of Iran related subjects.

There are a number of good one-volume histories of Iran now available for the general reader. Among the best are Michael Axworthy, *Empire of the Mind* (Penguin, 2008), and Homa Katouzian, *The Persians, Ancient, Medieval and Modern* (Yale, 2010). For those willing to be a little more adventurous the earlier English-language histories, especially John Malcolm (1815), offer some valuable insights. Malcolm spent some considerable time comparing and contrasting the mythical inheritance with the history as he understood it. He is refreshingly un-judgemental, and his memoirs of his time in Iran, entitled *Sketches of Persia*, published in 1827, remain one of the most acute observations of the Iranian character.

There are a number of translations of the *Shahnameh* available, though the best current abridgement and translation is by Dick Davis and published by Penguin. Davis has also published a translation of another epic poem, *Vis and Ramin* (Mage, 2013), as well as turning his attention to perhaps the most popular modern Persian novel, *My Uncle Napoleon* (Modern Library, 2006), a satire on the Iranian tendency to see 'the hand of the English' behind everything. Social and political satire has been a powerful tool for Iranian authors seeking to shed some light on the idiosyncrasies of their compatriots and a good example is the collection of short stories by Mohammad Ali Jamalzadeh, translated as *Once upon a time* (Mazda, 1985). The most famous satire was of course written by an Englishman and has had a profound influence on generations of foreign travellers who have occasionally forgotten that they have been reading a work of fiction. James Morier's *Hajji Baba of Isfahan* is a witty look at a peculiarly Iranian 'lovable rogue'. First published in 1824, it can lay claim to being among the first fictional bestsellers in the English-speaking world (it was the seriousness with which it was received that encouraged Malcolm among others to publish their own memoirs). The subsequent Persian translation proved equally successful in Iran until its English authorship was revealed.

There is a growing choice of books and articles on all aspects of Iran's history and politics, though comparatively few for the general reader that combine both scholarship and accessibility. Almost all the more recent popular 'windows' into contemporary Iran suffer from a tendency to accentuate the exotic and tend to view questions of Iranian history and identity almost exclusively through the prism of the Islamic Revolution, with often quite selective readings of the past in order to find the 'roots' of the present. The best scholarly synthesis for a more general readership remains Roy Mottahedeh's *The Mantle of the Prophet*, first published in 1985 and still in print. An excellent contemporary account, written by the Christian Science Monitor's Scott Peterson, a regular traveller to the country, is *Let the Swords Encircle Me* (Simon and Schuster, 2010). Those seeking more detail are encouraged to read histories of modern Iran by Abrahamian, Amir-Arjomand, and Amanat. Those interested in the bases for my own reading of Iranian history and identity should go to my *Politics of Nationalism in Modern Iran* (Cambridge, 2012).

Index

Iran

SOCIAL MEDIA
Very Short Introduction

Join our community
www.oup.com/vsi

- Join us online at the official Very Short Introductions
  Facebook page.
- Access the thoughts and musings of our authors with our
  online **blog**.
- Sign up for our monthly **e-newsletter** to receive information
  on all new titles publishing that month.
- Browse the full range of Very Short Introductions online.
- Read **extracts** from the Introductions for free.
- Visit our library of **Reading Guides**. These guides, written by our
  expert authors will help you to question again, why you think
  what you think.
- If you are a teacher or lecturer you can order inspection
  copies quickly and simply via our website.

ONLINE CATALOGUE
A Very Short Introduction

Our online catalogue is designed to make it easy to find your ideal Very Short Introduction. View the entire collection by subject area, watch author videos, read sample chapters, and download reading guides.

http://fds.oup.com/www.oup.co.uk/general/vsi/index.html

MODERN CHINA
A Very Short Introduction
Rana Mitter

China today is never out of the news: from human rights controversies and the continued legacy of Tiananmen Square, to global coverage of the Beijing Olympics, and the Chinese 'economic miracle'. It seems a country of contradictions: a peasant society with some of the world's most futuristic cities, heir to an ancient civilization that is still trying to find a modern identity. This *Very Short Introduction* offers the reader with no previous knowledge of China a variety of ways to understand the world's most populous nation, giving a short, integrated picture of modern Chinese society, culture, economy, politics and art.

'A brilliant essay.'

Timothy Garton, TLS

www.oup.com/vsi

ISLAMIC HISTORY
A Very Short Introduction
Adam J. Silverstein

Does history matter? This book argues not that history matters, but that Islamic history does. This *Very Short Introduction* introduces the story of Islamic history; the controversies surrounding its study; and the significance that it holds - for Muslims and for non-Muslims alike. Opening with a lucid overview of the rise and spread of Islam, from the seventh to twenty first century, the book charts the evolution of what was originally a small, localised community of believers into an international religion with over a billion adherents. Chapters are also dedicated to the peoples - Arabs, Persians, and Turks - who shaped Islamic history, and to three representative institutions - the mosque, jihad, and the caliphate - that highlight Islam's diversity over time.

'The book is extremely lucid, readable, sensibly organised, and wears its considerable learning, as they say, 'lightly'.'

BBC History Magazine